The Ultin Beginners Guide to Blowing Up on Instagram in 2019

How to Leverage Attention and the Power of Social Media Marketing to Create Your Personal Brand (Influencer Strategies)

Written by Dale Canzanelli

Dale Canzanelli

purposes only. All effort has been executed to present accurate, up to date, and reliable, complete information. No warranties of any kind are declared or implied. Readers acknowledge that the author is not engaging in the rendering of legal, financial, medical or professional advice. The content within this book has been derived from various sources. Please consult a licensed professional before attempting any techniques outlined in this book.

By reading this document, the reader agrees that under no circumstances is the author responsible for any losses, direct or indirect, which are incurred as a result of the use of information contained within this document, including, but not limited to, — errors, omissions, or inaccuracies.

3

Table of Contents

Introduction

I want to thank you for choosing this book, "The Ultimate Beginner's Guide to Blowing Up on Instagram in 2019: How to Leverage Attention and the Power of Social Media Marketing to Create Your Personal Brand."

Do you want to have a strong online presence? If that's the case, then you certainly aren't alone. All businesses, regardless of whether you are a small startup or a well-established player in the industry, use Instagram to market their business and increase their brand's presence. It is quite common to create a website and use common platforms like Facebook and Twitter. Almost everyone does this, but Instagram offers more than either of these platforms. If you want to reach 700 million active monthly users, then you need a good Instagram marketing strategy.

In this book, you will learn about Instagram, steps for getting started on Instagram, the benefits it offers, best practices to grow big on

Instagram, Instagram metrics and analytics tools and several other tips and tricks that will help increase your engagement on this rapidly growing platform.

So, if you are ready to learn more about making it big on Instagram, then let us get started without further ado.

Chapter 1: Instagram 101

About Instagram

Instagram is quite popular these days. It is one of the smartphone applications that has successfully managed to tap into the creative and image-dominated online presence of young people in the modern day. So much that in fact, it has become a buzzword. So, it is time that you are also up to speed about this app and what it's all about.

What is Instagram? To put it simply, it is a social networking application that allows users to share pictures and videos with others. It is a free application and is available for all operating systems. Two graduates from Stanford University, Kevin Systrom, and Mike Krieger, founded this company in 2010, and presently, it has over a billion users. Facebook acquired this platform in 2012. The primary idea of this platform is to enable picture sharing, but its popularity comes from its picture-editing features. Once you have a picture you want to post, then you can use various filters available on Instagram and the final image can look similar to an old Polaroid photograph. This app allows users to create personal and business profiles. Also, it can be linked to other social media sites like Facebook and Twitter. It essentially means that a user can now easily share the same content across multiple platforms.

It is not only a video- and a photo-sharing platform, but it also acts as a platform for brands and businesses to share their content with customers. Instagram is the perfect outlet for one's creativity to be shared with the world. Every image or video that is posted on Instagram covers the entire screen, and there is no space for any clutter. The inspiring, captivating, and engaging content offered is the main reason why people are drawn to Instagram.

Instagram's Reach

The use of mobile phones, as well as apps, have clearly surpassed the usage of any other form of online media in the United States. Instagram is quite popular among millennials and has over a billion active users, and this number is steadily increasing. In September 2013, Instagram had over 150 million users, and by March 2014, it had over 200 million users. This shows a steady growth of 66%, and these numbers are rapidly increasing. In fact, Instagram boasts over 20% of total Internet users worldwide. It is available in more than 20 different languages, and more than 60% of the total users reside outside the United States.

Did you know that over 60 million photos and videos are uploaded on this platform daily? This might shock you, but if you look at the demographics, you will get a better perspective about this statistic. On average, a user spends around 8 minutes per day on this social networking platform. Statistics show that more than 76% of teenagers are often active on it all day long. With more than 2 billion likes and 16 million comments per day, this platform shows brilliant user engagement. Are you still uncertain about what value Instagram will add to your life? If yes, then read on!

Benefits of Instagram

Here are all the benefits that Instagram offers.

It is more than a shiny toy

In this age of constant inventions, Instagram might seem like a new shiny toy. You might think that it is a new platform that an overhyped fad. Well, for starters, Instagram is no longer a new platform. It has been around for eight years, and its membership has been increasing continuously. This is a tried and tested platform. If the existing numbers are anything to go with, then its growth isn't likely to slow down any time soon.

All the "kids" are on it

There are several platforms that the "kids" (the

younger millennials) constantly use. Still, a lot of them use Instagram most. Why? Is it because their parents and other older relatives aren't on it like they are on Facebook? And guess where all these kids used to be initially? Yes, you guessed it right- Facebook. It is an evolutionary process. The younger generations keep looking for sites and then try to make them popular until everyone starts using it. Instagram is already the most popular social networking platform these days for businesses as well as individuals.

Photos and more photos

Why do you need to write paragraphs and paragraphs of text when you can simply post a picture? Instead of having to respond to a "what are you up to?" you can merely post a picture that shows what you are doing. Isn't that much easier and more informative? Pictures definitely convey more than words can - pictures show emotions, ideas, and a sense of reality. These are things that you cannot convey through text. Photos certainly bring the audience into your world, and it increases a bond of intimacy to make others also feel like they are a part of your life.

Also, when you think about photos from interaction, they are more engaging. For instance, look at your Facebook feed. What are the posts that grab your attention? Do you focus all your attention on all the text-filled posts or the ones with pictures in them? Usually, people tend to skim through texts and look at the photos. Now, imagine an entire feed filled with photos. It is certainly more entertaining and engaging.

Express your personality

Humans are social animals, and we all like to connect with others. Photos are a great means of self-expression. Photos precisely express your persona and all those who are behind a brand. For instance, a brand might post impromptu photos of its employees as a great way to connect with their audience. Regardless of what your personality is like, you can always find a way to express it on Instagram.

Marketer friendly

The creators of Instagram probably didn't plan for it, or even think that marketers would find their platform to be of good use. Using Instagram as a marketing tool is all the rage these days. It is quite easy for a business or a brand to place themselves in front of their desired audience. Instagram continues to come up with new features frequently, and all of these help marketers to market their brands or businesses. For instance, a brand can use the Instagram Live feature to unveil a new product or even live-stream an event. In the same manner, they can use Instagram Stories to give their viewers a behind-the-scenes look of what goes on in the business.

Ads

Instagram is a free service, and it is focused on users, but it doesn't mean that the platform isn't evolving. Instagram ads are the latest tool that social media marketers are using. It is quite similar to the promoted posts options on Facebook and Twitter. There are different formats in which ads can be presented - they can be specifically targeted for a certain audience, and there is no limit to how creative the ads can be. This is a great thing for all marketers out there; not just the marketers, but also all the individuals who are trying to market their brand. It is a great way for businesses to market to their ideal audience.

Tracking your analytics

One of the reasons why a lot of people love using Instagram for business is because it enables them to track their analytics. There are different metrics that one can use to understand how well their Instagram account is doing. For instance, if you want to be an influencer, then you must be aware of the right time to post and the kind of content you must post. All this will depend on your target audience; however, how will you know whether your current audience includes your target audience? The answer is quite simple.

You merely need to open Instagram analytics and check the performance of different metrics like the engagement, engagement rate, demographics and such. Once you have all this data on hand, you can devise your content strategy accordingly.

Chapter 2: Getting Started with Instagram

Start Using Instagram

Now that you are aware of how Instagram can add value to your life, the next step is to get started with Instagram. In this section, you will learn about the different steps that you must follow to start using the Instagram application.

Step One: Downloading the App

If you want to use Instagram, the most obvious step is to download it. Unlike its predecessor, Facebook, you need a mobile device to install this app. You can access the web version if you want, but certain features like analytics are only available on the mobile version.

Step Two: Select a Username

To sign up for Instagram, you can use your email address or even your Facebook account if you have one. After you do this, you will be prompted to select a username. I suggest that you must opt for a username that can be easily understood. After all, your username is how other users can find you on Instagram, and it will be the one that is displayed publicly on the Instagram account. If you are setting up an Instagram account for your business, then you have two options - either use the full name of your business, or the other option is to use an abbreviated version of the name so that other Instagrammers can easily find you with the help of Instagram's search function.

Step Three: Instagram profile

Now, you need to take some time to fill out the bio for your profile on Instagram. The bio has a text limit, so you need to come up with a clear and precise description of what your account is all about. If you opt for a specific niche, then the description must convey the same to viewers too. If you have a website, blog, YouTube channel or anything else, then feel free to add the URL to those socials in your bio. If your account is for a business, then add the business's address or location as well.

Step Four: Profile picture

As I have already mentioned, Instagram is a visual platform, and your profile isn't complete without a profile picture. The profile picture will be uploaded in a small circular frame in your profile. Ensure that your face or icon is visible in it. If you are trying to create a personal brand, then please ensure that you include your logo in the profile picture. The picture must be clear, and even though it will look like a small thumbnail, it must be clear and easily identifiable. If there are any other similarly named profiles, then your profile picture will help others identify you. If you want, you can always draw pictures from your other social media accounts and use it here. You can either upload a picture from existing ones on your device or take a new one using the app. As long as the picture is clear and relevant to your profile, you are good to go.

Step Five: Your first post

As soon as you set up your Instagram profile, it is time to get started. The first step is to post something. Yes, I am talking about your first post! As I have already mentioned, you can either go with an existing photo or take a new one using the app and upload it to your profile. Take some time to decide what your first post will look like. Instagram offers various features and filters that you can use to enhance the picture you are posting. Spend some time going through all of this. Once you have edited the picture and are happy with it, you need to post it. While posting it, ensure that you tag others in it. You can tag a location if you want to, but that's up to you.

Step Six: Inform others

If you are present on any other social networking platform, then you can inform others about your Instagram profile on those sites. If you don't do this, others will be oblivious about your existence on this platform. The simplest way to do this is by messaging your email or contact list about your new profile. To increase your online presence and visibility, you must inform others that you are on Instagram. Also, Instagram provides the option of syncing up your app to your contact list or your friend list on Facebook. If you do this, it will automatically suggest existing users from your list who are present on Instagram.

Step Seven: Start following other users

You need to start searching for others and following them. You can start by following similar accounts in your niche or industry. For instance, if you want your profile to be a fashion-oriented account, then ensure that you follow the influencers in your niche, as well as certain brands and critics. When you start following these people, then it prompts them to explore your account in turn. If it is a personal account, you can always ask your friends or those in your contact list for their usernames. You can also use hashtags to search for other users or related handles on Instagram. Instagram is all about networking, and to network, you must connect with your audience. Also, when you start exploring other pages, you might gain some insight and inspiration too.

Step Eight: Pictures, pictures, and more pictures

Well, those were the basics of Instagram. Now that you are following other users and have followers, you need to work on increasing your Instagram presence. The best and the easiest way to do this is by posting regularly. So, start posting pictures! You don't have to make up for lost time by posting hundreds of pictures at once. Start by posting maybe a picture or two per day. Don't forget to include tags, hashtags, and locations in your pictures.

Follow all the simple steps given in this chapter to create your Instagram account. Yes, it is as simple as that! You will learn more about building a strong Instagram profile in the next chapter. But for now, let's stick to the basics.

Tips for Beginners

Since you are just getting started with Instagram, there are certain essentials you must keep in mind. The list of dos and don'ts mentioned in this section will help you get a fair idea of what is and isn't desirable while using Instagram. After all, you do want to create your personal brand with this platform, don't you? These tips will come in handy when you are just getting started.

Start using hashtags

You might have come across Instagrammers using different hashtags. To increase your reach, engagement, and following on Instagram, you must use hashtags. Hashtags must not be used in a haphazard manner, and you must show some restraint and tact. Some people think that the more the better, and they tend to overstuff their captions with hashtags regardless of whether they are relevant or not. Please avoid making this rookie mistake. Ensure that you are only using hashtags that include the keywords related to your niche and are relevant. You will learn more about using hashtags later.

Photos as well as videos

If you want others to follow you, then you need to offer them something of value in return. After all, no one will want to waste their precious time following an account that is merely a waste of their time. Your posts must trigger some sort of emotion or feeling in the minds of the viewers. Try to make sure that your posts trigger emotions like love, nostalgia, or even humor. All this goes a long way in ensuring that your engagement rate stays high. Your followers will stick around only if they value the content you are sharing. Also, ensure that you are posting photos and videos. After all, this platform is visual media oriented.

Using filters

There is a wide array of filters to choose from on Instagram, and you can apply them to all your posts to make them more appealing. You might be tempted to use multiple filters, but don't go overboard, and keep your excitement in check. Using too many filters can completely distort the picture which you should. I suggest that you stick to images with a natural color and contrast composition. Instead of using too many filters, invest in a good camera. Pictures that look natural and aesthetically pleasing are the ones that do well.

About posting

You must keep posting interesting content, and you must do so regularly. You need to come up with fresh content regularly to keep things interesting. It doesn't mean posting ten pictures within 24 hours. It isn't only about posting - you must also ensure that your posts are engaging and interesting. If you want to hold onto your existing followers and acquire new ones, then you must keep things interesting. If your content is boring, not many followers will stick around. Also, if you don't post regularly, you will lose followers.

Interacting with your followers

Don't forget that Instagram is a social networking platform. As with any other social networking platforms, you must interact with your followers on the network. Don't ignore your followers who regularly engage with your content. Ensure that you reply to their comments and messages. You can ask for their feedback to strike up a conversation and acknowledge them. Everyone likes to know that they are acknowledged. A simple way in which you can do this is by replying to their comments. You can also view their profiles and like their posts to foster a bond with your audience.

Never purchase followers

Organic followers are always the way to go - don't ever purchase followers. It might be quite tempting during the initial stages to purchase followers to increase your reach, but that's a bad idea. Even if you do manage to obtain some followers for a low cost, it isn't effective. For instance, if you do buy Instagram followers, they will all be fake and inactive. Only the genuine Instagrammers are the ones who will effectively engage on Instagram, and if your followers are fake, you cannot expect any engagement from them. Also, it will look quite odd if you have thousands of followers in your account without any engagement (no comments or likes on your posts). Instead, it is a better idea to work on organically growing your follower base. You will learn about the various tips that you can follow to grow your followers. It might take a while, but it will certainly be worth your while.

Update yourself with the latest trends

Instagram keeps coming up with frequent updates. Therefore, it is quintessential that you ensure that you are always updated with the latest trends. Hashtags and shoutouts are certainly great, but they aren't part of the latest trends. So, pay attention to the latest trends, especially if you want to make it big on Instagram. If you don't do this, then you stand the risk of being left behind and can lose out on valuable following merely because you were unaware.

Instagram Direct

It is quintessential that you focus on the content you post as well as the frequency of the posts, but there is another thing that is equally important, and that's networking with your followers. You might wonder what the need for this is when your posts reach all your followers. Well, you must always target some of your most loyal followers and direct message them from time to time with some photos, videos or anything else that might be useful for them. Doing this ensures that your followers feel valued and appreciated. It is all a part of building your public relations. A simple way to go about this is by thanking them through direct messages for their support.

Search tab matters

The explore tab on Instagram is perhaps the most underappreciated feature Instagram offers. It enables you to explore various trending and popular posts as well as videos. This portion of Instagram is customized according to the engagement rate on pictures and videos that your followers engage with. It will certainly help you find new users to follow. Use this feature to check out your competition as well as any other new users in your niche. You will be able to understand the kind of topics that interest your followers. It will certainly come in handy if you want to design a social media marketing campaign.

Keep all these tips in mind while getting started and you will learn more about them in the coming chapters.

Chapter 3: Build a Strong Instagram Profile

In the previous section, you were introduced to basic steps that you must follow to create your Instagram account. In this section, you will learn about how you can build a strong Instagram profile for yourself.

The Perfect Instagram Name

Selecting the perfect name for your Instagram profile is a very important step. The name that you opt for must be simple. If you have a website, then ensure that the handle's name is similar to your website's domain name. This helps others recognize you immediately. It essentially means that your Instagram name must be something that instantly pops up in the search results and is easy to recognize. When you start thinking about different usernames for your account, you must design it in a way that gives viewers a good idea about your chosen niche. Please keep in mind that you aren't a popular brand or a celebrity, at least not yet! So, you must work on creating a profile that will help you gain followers. To achieve this objective, you need to have a username that isn't nondescript or obscure. Take a moment and think about it, how will your potential audience reach you if they aren't aware of you?

Before you finalize a username, take some time to learn about all the other users and businesses who failed at making it big on Instagram even before they took off. As mentioned, your username must give the viewers an idea of what they can expect from your account. You will immediately lose followers if they get disappointed or confused about the content you post. For instance, if your username suggests that they can get fashion advice about the latest trends and your recent posts are all about stock markets, then you will not be able to gain or retain any followers.

So, please don't rush finalizing a username. Instead, take a little time and consult others. You can do a little research to find the best names available in your niche. Look at your competitors for some inspiration. You can always ask your friends or family members for a second opinion. Select a name that fits your objectives and goes well with what you want your personal brand to be all about. There is a simple way in which you can determine the ideal name for your Instagram handle. Tell a few people about the name that you want to use and observe their initial reaction to it. This is the most genuine feedback you can ever get. Their reactions will tell you whether the name you want to opt for is any good or not. Here are a couple of aspects that all good usernames have.

Easy to pronounce

The name must obviously be easy to pronounce. If people cannot repeat it easily, then searching for your profile on Instagram will become quite a task. You must never opt for a name that users will not be able to remember without having to make a note of it. It must be easy to remember and pronounce. The name you opt for must not be ambiguous or confusing to others.

Uniqueness

It is obvious that you cannot use an existing username and no two usernames are ever alike. So, you must try to create one that is unique and doesn't share any similarities with other existing usernames. In any case, it is a terrible idea to copy an existing username or slightly tweak an existing username and use it for your account. If you do this, you can run into unnecessary legal trouble. If you don't want to get stuck with cases of copyright infringements, then please avoid doing this. Create a username that is unique!

Symbols

This is merely an extension of the previous tip. At times, you might need to use periods or underscores to make your username unique. It is a good idea to stay away from all these things, at least during the initial stages of growth of your account. Over time, you can certainly tweak the name of your account. Also, if you do want to use them, then limit them and don't ever place them consecutively. If you use too many periods or underscores, it becomes quite difficult for other Instagrammers to search for your account.

Short and sweet

A good username must always be short and simple. A long username is never a good idea. So, if you want supercalifragilisticexpialidociousgirl to be your username, then you might need to reconsider your decision. Yes, it certainly is unique, but it is quite a mouthful and difficult to remember as well as pronounce. Never opt for a complicated name, use a short and easy to pronounce username, it will automatically be easy to remember as well. Take a look at the Instagram handles of influencers in your niche and come up with a name accordingly. The username must always be short and precise. Shorter names also offer a certain degree of exclusivity.

Free of any bias

If you don't want to ruffle any feathers and want to have a rather smooth sailing experience, then ensure that your username is free from any bias. You must always remember that your audience will be quite diverse (can belong to different religions, genders, race, ethnicity...etc). So, keep all this in mind while selecting a username. If you select a name that seems biased towards a specific gender, race, religion or anything along these lines, then you are in for trouble. Please accept and respect the diversity of your followers.

No common names

Another important thing that you must keep in mind is that you need to avoid common words at all costs. While coming up with a username, try to avoid words like happy, business, billionaire or anything equally generic. Keep in mind that you will be competing with other established Instagram users and opting for a generic name will not help you.

Now that you are aware of the various tips that you can follow to create a good username, the next step is to put these tips into practice and come up with a name. Having a good username on Instagram will help increase your account's visibility.

The logo

If you aim to create a personal brand on Instagram, then you need a good logo. Don't worry even if you don't have a logo in mind at present. In fact, having a logo is very important for running a social media marketing campaign. If you do have a logo, then people will be able to associate your logo with your brand or business whenever they come across it. A logo is important for branding, especially if you are using social media to help with the growth of your business. A logo is an undeniable part of a brand's identity, and it helps all customers - potential as well as the existing ones, recognize your brand. Apart from all this, it gives your brand some recognition amongst your target audience. Seeing an attractive logo certainly sparks a sense of curiosity in the viewer and they will want to learn more about you.

Instagram Bio

It is quintessential that you understand the different components that are included in your Instagram bio. After you do this, you can add more information and improve your account so that users know what your brand is and what they can expect while following you. The main problem you encounter when creating a bio is the lack of free space. The Instagram section for your bio only allows 150 characters. Your username should be no more than 30 characters. With over 800 million active users in the app, you should maximize your chances of discovery and follow an effective marketing strategy. In this section, you will learn about different things that you need to keep in mind in order to create a brilliant bio on Instagram.

Profile picture

Your Instagram profile page should contain a profile photo that is related to your business or brand. The photo you are using may be a logo or a photo of the product. Whatever you choose as a profile photo should be attractive, and the viewer should easily be able to associate it with your business. As a rule, many companies, celebrities, brands, and influential people use a proven icon on their profile to identify themselves.

A feature of Instagram is that the profile picture is cropped in a circle. This means that your profile picture is visible, and you need to make sure that it remains clear and visible after trimming. You do not need to worry about loading a square-shaped photo with a photo of your brand or a logo in the center as the corners are trimmed without trimming the branding.

Username and name

Both username and name can be searched in the Instagram search field. The username is displayed at the top of your Instagram profile; it is quite noticeable in bold. As mentioned earlier, it is important to choose a username and a name carefully. If you have a simple and short name, search results can easily show your profile. After searching, the name will be displayed in gray under the profile handle.

Public profile

You need to make sure your Instagram descriptor is public and not private. In fact, you shoot yourself in the foot if your profile is configured as a personal account. If your profile is a personal account, any visitor to your profile will not be able to see any of the photos you have published. It instantly will not allow people to follow you. To prevent this from happening, all you need to do is make sure that you go to your account settings and disable the "Personal Account" setting. If you have a business profile on Instagram, the default is a public account.

Bio

The bio contains a brief description and a summary of you and your business. Many companies use this space to list the products or services they offer, the URL of their website, their location, and their physical address. You must keep your bio short and sweet because you only have 150 characters to convey everything you want.

Website

You can include the URL of your website in your bio to increase the visibility of your business and encourage those who visit your profile to visit the business site for more information. In this field, be sure to add a link to your site. Finally, you need a landing page that you can use to direct all traffic.

Category

This feature is only available for business accounts. The category is displayed under the company name and is directly linked to the category selected on the corresponding Facebook page. For example, if you indicate that you are a restaurant or public person, simply select the appropriate category.

Call-to-action buttons

To enable the call-to-action buttons, you must enter the required information, such as email address, phone number, and location. Previously, business account users entered their email address and address in the "Bio" section. This feature has been added for business accounts that have been set up to free up bio space. Note that this feature is displayed only in the application view and not in the web view. You can find this feature by going to the 'Edit Profile' option and selecting 'Contact Options.'

Email

If you add an email address in the bio, an email button will be created in your profile. Whenever someone clicks on an email option, the application instantly opens the default email application on their device. This makes it easy for your followers and potential customers to communicate with you via email.

Recently, Instagram has also released a new feature that allows you to use hashtags and profile links in your bio. It offers marketers various ways to use hashtags. For example, if your brand has different Instagram markers for different aspects of your business, you can refer to other markers in your bio, rather than your subscribers looking for them. This will certainly make it easier to search for your transactions, especially if your accounts have not yet been verified.

You can increase your visibility and relevance by understanding how you can make the most of the various components of your bio. A good bio makes more sense to your followers.

How do you write a bio?

The Instagram bio informs followers and other

Instagrammers about the nature of their business. In essence, this is a brief description of yourself. To make an impression, the bio must be concise and memorable. A catchy bio can make people follow you and encourage them to do business with you. If your main goal is marketing on Instagram, make sure that you have developed an amazing bio. Here are a few things you need to create a brilliant bio.

Add a slogan

If you want to captivate your bio, you must use the slogan. The slogan in a few words shows the audience what your company is about. In addition, you can also use a summary of your company's values or add a mission statement to your bio.

Be minimalistic

The perfect bio on Instagram is always short and simple. You must provide all the information your target customers need to understand the main purpose of your brand. You do not need to fill out your bio with a lot of information, but rather stick to the main components. Finally, a visitor can browse your Instagram posts or visit your website to learn more about your business.

Link your account

This will improve your bio's effectiveness and help you with this. You can link your Instagram account to your Facebook, Twitter, and Snapchat accounts so your subscribers can easily find your business on other social networking platforms. It increases your reach and increases visibility on the Internet.

Hashtags

The hashtag allows other Instagram users to share their content with you in their feed. The user can use your hashtag and improve interaction with your audience. It also helps create a compelling brand story. So, if you have a brand hashtag, you need to include it in your bio.

Branded hashtags are not limited to products, and you can also purchase them for the services you offer. For example, service providers can combine emoji and hashtag tags to create a feed that will humanize their brand and make it more attractive. Please note that interactive hashtags are only available in the Instagram web interface, and not in the mobile application.

Use Emoticons

Using emoticons (emojis) can help the user convey a brand's personality. Otherwise, emoticons can be used as an alternative to certain words, and you can create space in your bio. Emojis also make Instagram posts and the bio more exciting.

Emojis are pretty cute, and it is good to use them often, but it is also a good idea to integrate them into the Instagram toolkit. From the faces to the animals and other characters - each emoticon you choose will create a sense of brand identity. Emojis can say more than a thousand words and helps you say more about your brand than words can. In fact, you can effectively communicate with Emojis and reduce the number of words used. It will also help create space in your bio. Emojis are good and have a certain appeal, but you have to remember that you should not overuse emoticons. Do not fill out your bio with smileys, because not all viewers play Pictionary.

Use line breaks

Using line breaks in the Instagram bio is a prime example of your skills and capabilities on Instagram. Moreover, it makes the profile more attractive and convenient to use. Line breaks help break up information into small pieces that are easily read by visitors. It will also help you highlight the most important things in your business.

Add a call-to-action

When creating the perfect bio, keep in mind that you cannot avoid a real call-to-action. Without a request for action, your bio is incomplete. The call-to-action should encourage your audience to visit your online store, access your website, or call or email you for more information. Ask yourself what exactly visitors should do after displaying your profile before making a decision.

For example, you might want people to like your Facebook page, subscribe to a newsletter, order products directly from your website, or take action appropriate to your marketing goals. You should be aware when asking your visitors and potential customers to take concrete action. Do not tell them to do something that prevents them from following you or dealing with you. For example, if you want to create an episode on Instagram, ask your visitor to follow your channel.

Include contact information

It is very important to ensure you have contact information in your bio. Imagine that you have an individual who is impressed with your company and wants to contact you, but does not have contact. You will need to include your contact information in your bio. This can be a phone number or an email address. Instead of just posting comments in messages, users can contact you directly.

What makes you unique?

What makes you unique when compared to all the other accounts in your niche? If you are certain that there is something that sets you apart from the rest, then ensure that you include the same tidbit in your bio and you will see a difference.

A good Instagram profile must describe perfectly what you and your business are about.

Follow all these steps, and you can quickly create an interesting and inspiring bio on Instagram. The only thing that you should never forget when creating a bio is a character limitation.

Chapter 4: Instagram Tactics

Now that you have the perfect Instagram account, the next step is to concentrate on growing and promoting your account so that you reach your target audience. I suggest that you carefully go through all the steps given in this chapter - from creating your account to building awareness and improving your brand's narrative. All these tricks will enable you to understand how you can build your account so that you can reach a wider audience. In this section, you will learn about the following:

Set up the perfect account

If you want to create an Instagram account, you must first choose a name that is recognizable and short. You can use the brand name or indicate the region you are targeting. For example, Mercedes-Benz uses "@mbusa" as the username for an Instagram account that is related to the USA. For a profile picture, it is best to use a graphic icon or a recognizable brand, such as a logo.

The next step is to develop a brief and interesting bio about the brand and add a link to your main site or another campaign site. This is the only place where you can redirect traffic. Therefore, it is important that the hyperlink included in the bio directs users to the desired landing page.

Create awareness

Instagram is an art platform based solely on images. If you take this into account, you will be able to identify influential individuals who are guided by your brand's values. It is important to analyze the composition and style of photos and videos that these influential people use to connect to your audience.

Only when you have quality content will it trigger the awareness of your subscribers. It is important to create a solid foundation that will be beautiful and innovative. This contributes to the success of your brand on social networking sites. You have to remember that viewers use Instagram to view original and beautiful content. They are not interested in advertising campaigns. It is very easy for a user to open a brand. It is important that you strive for at least one high-quality post every day.

Contests and Campaigns

If you are running contests or campaigns, it's better to use Instagram as you can reach a large audience. This platform simplifies the whole process for users who use hashtags. You can tailor campaigns and make them more attractive using the Instagram application programming interface (API), which increases the number of options. Any content created by users can be viewed and used effectively. When awarding prizes, it is best to scale the price in accordance with the obligations given by users. If a lot of effort is required, it is best to award prizes that increase the quality and quantity of user input.

It is always useful to use contests to get custom

content. One of the easiest and most common contests is the Like and Comments contest. Users can comment on and like photos or videos that you have posted on your brand page in hopes of winning the contest. They participate in a competition that lasts for a short period. You can use the API to keep track of entries and contact the winners. You can do a different version of this contest by asking users to take a picture or use a specific hashtag. If you are dependent on the future usage of custom content, be sure to install unique hashtags that are easy to view.

When you start to attract an audience, analyze them, and work with likes and comments, you build relationships between your brand and the user or consumer. If you use original content, you can expand your reach. If you are using consumer content, it's best to get permission from the creator to avoid plagiarism. When you finish the competition, it is best to create a post in which the materials submitted by the winners will be presented. This will lead to more users in future competitions or campaigns.

Maintain relationships

If you're in the Instagram community, you can increase brand awareness. You will recognize the brand community better when you follow brand partners, supporters, representatives. If you want to socialize with users and increase your brand awareness, it's best to contact the above users. When it comes to managing the community, it has little effect, since most conversations and meetings occur because of likes; however, if you are tracking and responding to comments, you can continue the conversation.

It is always nice to reward subscribers for staying true to your brand. If you give them simple benefits such as discounts, coupon codes, free gifts, and product samples, you will leave an indelible impression. If this works, you can use it as an advertising strategy.

Community management is a process that occurs when creating high-quality content. Since

Instagram is an image-based platform, the bulk of communication happens when you create and share innovative and attractive content as a brand.

Developing Interesting Content

If you want to measure the effectiveness of content, you need to study two criteria - reach and engagement. It is important to track other data, but the above indicators are key performance indicators that can help evaluate the performance of brands on Instagram.

Reach denotes the total number of people who have seen all the content posted on your brand page. Wonderful and interesting content will get more attention on the "Search on Instagram" tab, which will increase the number of views, which will in turn increase coverage. By installing tests, you can improve the content you publish and increase the number of subscribers overnight. In this way, you can create content that matches your brand. If your profile has hundreds of views, you can attract more people to follow your brand, increasing your reach.

Participation in Instagram is measured by the number of likes and comments on the post. Comments often include a hashtag that helps measure the activity of the target community. Different types of information can be tracked, for example, filters and their effectiveness, content, and style of content that has attracted the most attention. It is best to use trial and error to track engagement and set benchmarks that will help improve the quality of your brand's content.

You will learn in detail about all these steps in the coming chapters.

Chapter 5: How to Grow Big on Instagram

In this section, you will learn about the different tips you can follow to help you grow on Instagram.

Niche Matters

Instagram is growing and is currently one of the most popular social networking sites. As an entrepreneur or marketer, you need a niche Instagram account if you want to reach your target audience. If you want to reach your target audience, you must first define your niche. This will help you find a large fan base, and you will also develop a successful marketing strategy.

Many people usually join Instagram to chat and have fun. It provides a platform where you can share your personal photos and interact with others. In addition, it is also an effective tool that you can use as part of your marketing strategy. Many users usually do not know that they can use this platform to increase the visibility of their business. Your visibility will be increased if you can identify a niche. Instagram's most popular niches today include fashion, health and fitness, travel and tourism, and beauty. It should not be a problem if your business does not fall under one of these niches. Start by assessing the most appropriate niche for your business that will make you unique.

Currently, you can find a niche on Instagram for almost anything you want - whether it's food blogging, travel marketing, or even succulent breeding. If you have something that you find interesting, you will probably find others who are interested. You must find a niche and stick to it. Finding your niche may not be easy, but here are a few things you can do to find your niche for yourself and your Instagram brand.

Discover yourself

To find a niche on Instagram, you must first ask yourself what interests you. Most preferably, it should be what you love. Maybe you have a passionate interest in beauty. This means that you can choose a beauty niche on Instagram. It is desirable to have a niche that you are passionate about. It can be a very costly commitment to invest in a niche that you don't like. If you do, there is a chance that you will quickly lose interest, or you will get bored and change your mind.

Before you choose a niche, it's time to get a little lost. Even if it sounds like a cliché, it will help you find what you find passionate. If you are not sure about the right niche, you can always contact your friends or family members and consider their opinions.

Color Scheme

When it comes to a niche on Instagram, first impressions always matter. People only need half a second to decide whether to follow you or not. You can always make an impression by constantly using the right assortment of colors.

Some people tend to be passive users, especially during busy hours of the day. If you want to make them follow you, you must engage them on your profile at first glance. Most likely, people view your profile through a small grid format before deciding to follow you.

You can do a small survey to learn the most popular colors. You can do this in a discreet way, which only involves creating a color scheme and then recognizing feedback according to different color schemes. Thus, you can find a color scheme that will delight your users.

First, you can use different styles of photography, such as minimal, rich, black and white, landscape, or portrait. This will help you determine the style of photography that appeals to your audience the most. If you have not yet reached the initial stage of finding your subscribers, stick with this, because you may lose subscribers who are only interested in your style.

Consistency

Being consistent is a robust approach that will ensure the credibility of your niche. Adding trust to your brand through Instagram is like blogging. It requires consistency in posting new content to be creative and to inform its subscribers when to expect the next update from you. If you want to create your own niche with frequent posts, you can use the Instagram function.

In lieu of this feature, avoid posting more often than once every 6 hours. In addition, do not post more than three times a day. Publish and manage your content wisely and do not spam your subscribers. By doing this, you quickly lose followers.

Engaging and Entertaining Content

If you want to increase the number of subscribers on Instagram, you need to create attractive content and images. Creating high-quality images and content takes time, effort, perseverance, and dedication. In this section, you'll learn about various tips that you can use to create high-quality images and content that will improve your profile on Instagram.

Understand your target audience

If you have a content creation strategy, you must remember your audience, who can see, hear, or view content. Never forget that the key to creating effective content is not focusing on topics that you personally like, but the type of content your audience will enjoy. Finally, the goal of Instagram Marketing is to increase your reach and widen your audience. Before creating content, you must first determine the type of audience to which you want to access. You cannot create perfect content if you do not know much about your audience. Therefore, you must develop a content marketing strategy that solves the most pressing problems of your audience. You should try to educate and transform your audience. To learn more about your audience, you need to interact with them, view their personal preferences, and apply them when creating content. The content you create should be directly related to your audience. Therefore, you must be empathetic and understand what your audience is going through.

Diversify your content

If you want to create engaging content, you should never be limited to any particular means of communicating with your audience. You must change the content in each post to diversify it. If you usually write text blogs, you should include some videos, pictures, quotes, graphics and the like. Think about different ways to add humor to your content. Try to spice up your content at times.

Better pictures

Adding images to your profile will increase the trust and legitimacy of your product. You cannot do this if you do not have the appropriate photos. If you want to use photos, make sure you use a high-quality camera. You can also use your smartphone to take good pictures. Images must be of high quality and relevant to the content that you publish. You must agree with the main purpose of your brand.

Edit pictures

After selecting a specific photo, you need to edit it for the best effect. Even without a computerized photo editor, you can use free mobile apps that are available to improve the quality of your photos. Instagram also has certain filters that you can use to improve the quality of your photos. With photo editing software, you can turn a regular image into a well-defined infographic. Infographics are a great way to make content more attractive.

Focus on Contrast and Balance

The picture must have the right contrast to highlight it in the Instagram feed. Contrast can include colors, fonts, lighting, exposure, scaling, and gaps. You need to find the right scale that underlines the picture.

Insert quotes in photos

Currently, photos with embedded quotations are a trend, and they have become a popular tool for increasing interest and reaction on Instagram. You can use a famous quote, and then place it on the photo. Good deals are easily available online. The only thing you need to keep in mind is that the pictures and quotes you use correspond to the purpose of your brand.

Leave spaces and borders for pictures

You can create an unusual effect on the image by placing white edges around the images on Instagram. This has a better effect than the normal limit and is quite attractive. Make sure that the elements in your design have a place to be noticeable. This is an important aspect that you should consider avoiding overloading the message.

Keep these things in mind, and you will be able to create engaging content.

Chapter 6: Being Transparent on Social Media

If you want to build and maintain relationships with your existing and potential customers, you need to be transparent with your target audience. If you want to gain trust, you must be honest and keep your promises. It is important to appreciate transparency when interacting with the audience on social networks. Many people do not understand how important it is to be transparent with their audience and what impact this has on the marketing campaign. Transparency helps you create a large fan base on Instagram and increase your marketing strategy and profitability.

Creating business pages on Instagram allows you to build open relationships with your customers. This transparency reflects your business ethics, and also helps to acquire and maintain a base of loyal customers. In this section, you will learn how important transparency is in social networking.

Increases Customer Loyalty

Most of your subscribers could be customers who need better customer service. In customer relations, transparency makes a significant contribution towards increasing customer confidence and loyalty. This may take time, but with constant and careful effort you will eventually conquer the hearts of existing and potential customers with transparency. To be transparent costs nothing. All you need to do is keep good communication and customer problem-solving. Honesty and integrity are the cornerstones of a fruitful relationship.

In addition to creating a customer base and selling products, your Instagram page can help you increase brand loyalty. What exactly does brand loyalty mean? If you constantly provide valuable and interesting content, your subscribers will remain loyal and not notice your mistakes. Nowadays, people want to find companies to shop at, and often search for on social networks. If your subscribers see that your brand or business is very active and responsive on the Internet, they are more likely to deal with you than a company with no Instagram presence or a poorly managed website. In the age of technology in which we live in, the Internet has become an important part of our lives. Social networks have become a convenient substitute for real-time conversations. People tend to go to social networks for opinions about different things. If your brand is present in social networks, your chances to win over new customers and keep the existing ones are higher.

Enhances Reputation

The brand and reputation of the company will grow with increasing transparency. Satisfied customers will surely tell others about the experience they have with your brand. A satisfied customer is the best tool for advertising. If someone is happy with their experience with your brand, they will probably recommend it to others. This word-of-mouth advertising can make a big difference and help you in your marketing campaign.

Obtains Feedback from the Audience

Thanks to transparency, the relationship between your company and your subscribers opens the door to honest and open communication. Customers will be ready to give their suggestions and feedback when you are receptive, and if you respond positively to criticism and make the necessary changes, your audience will feel valuable. They will be happy to help you make the necessary changes to overcome any potential flaws in your brand. An honest review of your products or services, even if the reviews are not necessarily positive, can help you make changes to your brand. Of course, you can get new ideas from the reviews of your followers on Instagram.

Evidence in social networks is very important for any business. The number of likes, promotions, and comments you receive will help increase your online presence. It also gives you the confidence you need to work on a wider range of products or services. All these likes and promotions can also help you judge whether the public approves or not.

Improves Customer Service

Transparency is essential for good customer relationship practices. Taking into account feedback from followers of social networks and giving a timely response can be helpful in improving customer service. It gives them the feeling of being heard and appreciated. Thus, take the time to collect, survey, and process feedback received online. After all, your followers act only on the basis of transparency and freely express their thoughts.

Increases Follower Confidence in your Business

This particular advantage of transparency is hardly worth mentioning because of its obviousness. Consumers trust companies that are open and honest with them, even on social networks. With the advent of social networks, including Instagram, it is important to manage the image of the business. Transparency and a high level of trust from customers and subscribers in social networks mean that companies can cope with all problems much better because they have a chance to get a personalized solution. Clients and subscribers on social networks will be less likely to come to conclusions when problems occur and will wait until the company can respond.

If you want to play a big role in the world of social media marketing, you need to be open and transparent when working with clients and other users. This increases trust and loyalty and ultimately becomes a significant incentive for your marketing campaign.

Chapter 7: Use Stories

If you want to share your Instagram adventures with all your followers, you need to use Instagram stories. This is better than uploading an image and offers several options for updating photos or videos that you want to share. Make sure your ad campaign meets the latest updates and Instagram features.

Stories from Instagram are very similar to news feeds, but the only difference between them is that the first one is more visual. It allows the user to add various filters and effects to the camera, and you should post them in the "Stories" section, rather than upload them like regular publications. Stories that you create on Instagram can be shared with a group of people or even a single user. If you publish an article, it will be available within 24 hours and then disappear. This is very similar to the Snapchat story.

To prepare your photos for Instagram stories,

you have three options. Open the Instagram app on your phone, tap the "Your Story" icon, and then tap the camera icon in the upper left corner of the screen. You will need to press the record button to take a photo or video. If you want to share an existing photo, you can download it from the camera. If you want your brand or business to feel fashionable and cool, you should be aware of new developments that they constantly present.

The Instagram Story feature is a clone of the Snapchat Story. You must make sure that you are familiar with this practice before you decide to use it on your business page. The first thing you need to do is to do a survey before using the feature. Check out all the different buttons and their functions, and then do a quick test drive.

As an entrepreneur, you are a representative of your business, and your contribution to Instagram should reflect the same thing in not only your messages but also your stories. You need to make sure that the smilies, filters, colors, borders, text colors, and hashtags you use are brand-oriented. Try to present your brand voice in a fun and creative way.

You need to regularly and often publish stories from Instagram. Instagram Stories gives you a quick look at everything that happens to you and your business. So, if you want to provide interesting information to your subscribers and friends, select stories on Instagram, you need to take into account the time when most of your subscribers are online, and then publish them accordingly. You can also add a story at any time. You must make sure that the content you upload reaches your audience or else it will defeat the purpose altogether.

Remember that all your followers can view the Stories you post. Stories are an easy way for most people to establish a personal connection with the audience. So, remember that it is about creating a personal connection, without putting you in a business mess. You need to find the perfect balance between business and personal communication. Share some posts that are interesting or easy, and click about business in some posts.

Your Instagram followers are always looking for something genuine and authentic. You are a representative of your company, but do not forget to convey to the audience something that will make them dependent. With Instagram Stories you can maintain and improve your relationships with online users. To make the stories look a bit more unique, you can add selfies, post photos about interesting parts of your day, give an idea of the processes within your business, or even add quotes or "deep thoughts." For example, if you have a big ad or a big event planned for the future, you can use Instagram Stories for daily updates on this topic.

The only thing you should never forget when using advertising on Instagram is that people switch to Instagram because it is fun and interesting for them. So, you need to make sure your Instagram stories match these simple criteria. The best way to make people look forward to your updates is to offer them something of value. You need to entertain them, give them an understanding that they cannot get from anyone else, share things that make them feel valuable, and give them a personal view of your business, which can be done through Instagram stories.

Now that you know your Instagram stories, you need to integrate them into your marketing campaign successfully.

How to Use Instagram Stories

Instagram stories are a great way to increase your fan base; however, some people do not know how to use this feature to find fans on Instagram. There are several tactics you can use for Instagram stories.

Generate curiosity

The best application of Instagram Stories is to use it to generate curiosity amongst your followers. While posting the story, ensure that you end it on a cliffhanger. When you end something on a cliffhanger, you automatically make the viewer curious about what's coming next. In fact, a lot of popular series use this to increase the curiosity in their audience. For instance, the previous season of Game of Thrones ended on such a cliffhanger that people have been eagerly waiting for over a year for the next season to premiere. So, when you end the story on a cliffhanger, you must tell the viewers that if they want to know what happens, they will need to wait for the next story or post. Thus, you will be able to create an audience that is thoroughly interested and will be naturally inclined to view the next thing you post. If you fail to post the next segment, then it will only dissatisfy your audience and you will quickly lose followers.

Select a Theme

Experts on social networking have always suggested that you have a theme on an Instagram page. The most important part of your story is to stick to your niche. For example, you cannot be in fashion and tell a series of stories about your trip to a chic restaurant. This will be a general connection, and your audience will not see the full connection. One thing is certain: if you stick to a theme, you can attract people who share your love for that particular topic. Thus, you will develop your fanbase.

Story Viewing

People like to see pictures in stories. Otherwise, they get bored as soon as they read content that does not contain images. According to a study to determine the effect of images on reader literacy, single-page single-image content can increase reading motivation by 35 percent. With Instagram stories, this is no different. No matter how many stories you want to publish on your page, make sure that you add at least one appropriate image.

Use color and contrast to your advantage

Ideal Instagram posts are brighter and full of

blue, gray, and green. This contrasts with oversaturated posts that are fainter and full of yellow, pink and orange hues; however, it is useful to know which colors your viewers prefer. Therefore, keep your story bright, and all eyes will be on you. In fact, you can even add a color palette as part of your design.

Avoid filters

Even if it is known that filters make photos gorgeous, it is a modest practice to use photos in their original form; however, this requires the use of a high-quality camera. According to the most experienced experts on social networks, content on Instagram without filters will give the best results. If you have a high-resolution camera, the image will be better. You do not need to use the filter function. Therefore, if you have an image of the last 24 hours that has already been filtered, stick with the original. In fact, you can start creating Instagram Stories that can display your antics for the day or give a glimpse to your audience about what you have been up to all day long. An entire story made up of these episodes can give viewers a look behind the scenes, giving them an unfiltered look at your life.

Be dedicated and publish regularly

As a proven method for social networks, you should publish stories and posts regularly. Once you start posting Stories at a certain time regularly, ensure that you stick to that schedule. It might be a simple tactic to generate curiosity or maintain consistency. If you want to ensure that your followers are still interested in viewing your Stories, then you must posy Stories regularly to avoid losing them.

Thus, if your last post is hidden in all channels, people will start to forget you. It seems the consensus is that you have to create one story per day. Since the stories are short-lived, you should post a photo along with a Story every day.

Chapter 8: Growing your Fanbase

After creating an Instagram page and communicating with Instagram subscribers, it is a good idea to develop a strategy to reach a wider audience. Essentially, you need to know how to get a huge fan base without being known to anyone outside the Instagram community.

You will also want to find out how to get more free Instagram followers. One of the safest ways is through shout-outs. If you want to master this remarkable tendency to build subscribers, your website will become popular in a matter of weeks or months.

In fact, shout-outs are a form of advertising for other sites, created mainly by authoritative pages and authoritative users. In general, a shout-out refers to when a famous Instagrammer mentions you in his account and then orders his fans or subscribers to browse and follow you. Shout-outs are a great way to put your name in front of a large number of users and potential subscribers. Unfortunately, it is not so easy to get approval from the constantly busy (and potentially expensive) influential person and well-known Instagrammers. It requires networking and constant contact with popular accounts. In some cases, you may also be ready to publish the content of other users as part of a support agreement in your feed.

Time is important when it comes to shout-outs. On Instagram, shout-outs have to have a large audience for them to be effective. Even if you cannot dictate terms to those you want to help you, ask them to create a shout-out at a specific time. This requires that you investigate and understand when most people are online.

Currently, well-known users of social networks, including famous Instagrammers, are referred to as influential people. These people have big fans on their social media platform. People who follow these people are usually devoted to their content, opinions, and ideas. Because of the difficulty of making the right purchasing decision, some people rely on recommendations from friends and family members. In social networks, potential buyers increasingly rely on recommendations from influential people on Instagram and other social networking stars. As a company or business, you can use famous Instagrammers to promote your website and your products.

Many people have strange beliefs when it comes to appealing to an influential person. For example, some believe that influential individuals are turning to brands, and not vice versa. It's true that powerful Instagram users make the first decision about whether to accept or sell a product or service of a particular brand. If you like the product or the main purpose of the page, contact the company and ask them to work with you. Instagrammers can still promote a brand without a direct partnership.

Although this is possible, it is usually companies

that turn to Instagram Influencers to promote their brands. They ask them to test a new product line and see if they can integrate it into their marketing strategy or not. You don't have to wait for powerful Instagram people to contact you, as this may never happen. These are people who follow a rigid schedule and do not even have a minute to spare to look for people.

Another way to become an influential Instagrammer is to connect through a platform that is on every social networking platform. In particular, most well-known people on Instagram believe that the best connection with brands is through the influence platform. The platform provides neutral space for third parties, where powerful individuals and brands can meet and discuss their way. The platform allows brands to discover new and growing influential people and vice versa. Most of the platform is governed by conditions that properly regulate the behavior of both parties. This gives some confidence in how transactions between powerful individuals and brands are handled.

How can you come across influencers on Instagram? The best way to search for them is by using Instagram's search tab and trending hashtags. You can also find them on other influencer blogs or communities. Make a list of some of the most trending hashtags in your niche and then look up the most popular search results. This will help you find the influencers in your niche.

Having connected to the existing client base, you can also find out whom they are following and listening to on social networks. For example, if a large number of your clients follow a specific makeup Instagrammer, connect with that person and use them as an influence.

It's fair to offer incentives to influential Instagram users who promote your brand and/or product. First, politely contact them before asking to promote your website or product. After establishing an ideal relationship, you can offer them content or ask them to familiarize themselves with the products or services. In short, there are several approaches to interact with influential individuals to promote your brand or product.

Increase your Subscribers

When you first start on Instagram, it's interesting to imagine how many followers can access your account - more than one billion users. The truth is, your first 10,000 Instagram followers are the hardest to get. The main reason for this is that no one knows who you are yet. They still have a long way to go to establish themselves as a successful brand and an influential person; however, this does not necessarily mean that it is impossible. In a short time, it is possible to have a large number of subscribers, if you follow the right guidelines. Here are some tips to help you reach 10,000 Instagram subscribers in a month.

Choose a Topic

By choosing a theme for your Instagram page,

you can participate in a niche community. Moreover, you can make a name for yourself. In addition, themes can encourage Instagram users to follow you. If you know that you are posting consistent and similar content to an image or publication that you originally opened and that you enjoy as well as your audience, you should click "follow." Most people in your audience will search for other pages.

Join Instagram Interaction Groups

Are you just starting to find followers on Instagram? This strategy is best for beginners. Some newcomers to Instagram have seen their Instagram subscribers grow faster than expected, so they all ask what makes them different. The fact is, they joined engagement groups.

While it may be difficult to join the largest groups for engagement on Instagram, you will get a more accurate list of subscribers on Instagram by staying in your niche. You can easily find Instagram interaction groups for travel, beauty, and fashion among other niches. From these groups, you can get subscribers and preferences from people whose interests are similar to yours; however, if you want to get serious about garnering attention, you must also return the favor by following fan pages for people who join the group. Another way to become an influential Instagrammer is to connect through a platform that, obviously, is on every social networking platform. In particular, most popular people on Instagram believe that the best connection with brands is through the influence platform. The platform provides a neutral space for third parties, where powerful individuals and brands can meet and discuss a working relationship. The platform allows brands to discover new and growing influential people and vice versa. Most of the platform is governed by conditions that properly regulate the behavior of both parties. This gives some confidence in how transactions between powerful individuals and brands are handled.

Join Instagram Interaction Groups

Despite the fact that it is difficult to participate in large groups to interact on Instagram, you will receive a more detailed list of Instagram subscribers who are part of your niche. You can easily find Instagram interaction groups for travel, beauty, and fashion among other niches. Even if it is not conducive to an immediate sale, your brand may gain credibility in advance. It is important to note that this is a short-term strategy. It should be used to get Instagram subscribers only within the first weeks on Instagram, and not in the long run.

Choose the right content on Instagram

To attract the attention of a large number of real people on Instagram, you must create content. This should be done not only specifically for Instagram but also to properly adapt to what your audience wants. When creating content, it is very important to find the right approach and style. This is because your content will become what will be recognized by your subscribers.

In general, there are several types of images that work well with many niches. Posters with inspirational or humorous quotes, high-quality food photography, or pictorial images are a safe starting point for your content creation strategy. It is advisable to examine what content you produce carefully. Always acknowledge that Instagram is a hit because it is a completely unique platform. It provides user interaction that is different from other social networks. In short, create unique content for your Instagram account.

Produce Content Your Audience Will Love

If you know what content suits your brand, focus on creating exceptional posts that you know are related to your audience. This may seem obvious, but many marketers and influential individuals have neglected the creation of content. Find out what your customers appreciate on Instagram or what topics they are connected to. Then you can fill your account with relevant content.

In any case, you need to contact your audience. Do not forget the saying that beauty is in the eye of the beholder. That is why it is so important to build good relationships with your audience and find out what content they like. There have been several cases when people published something that, in our opinion, would increase involvement in general.

To make sure you create great content, you need to find out what your competitors are publishing. Also, know what type of images are used on their websites or blogs that are popular and simulated in your industry. Do not copy or paste!

Ask Customers to Share their Photos

If you are starting with an Instagram marketing strategy, it's much easier to find Instagram followers with photos of customers in your feed. It does a lot to increase social proof.

After you have made several sales, contact your customers and offer a free gift or incentive to get high-quality images using the product they purchased. Of course, providing incentives should not be a long-term strategy, but a short-term one. This should help you grow your brand.

Have a Single Style

This sounds like one of those inadequate approaches to getting followers on Instagram. This is not the case. Social media marketing experts believe that people do not follow a page due to published content; instead, they follow a page because they think the future content will be. What they expect in the future is the consistency of the style of the content that excites them right now.

Getting used to a consistent style is more than just branding. It's also about creating a wait for your Instagram account that your subscribers or potential subscribers can rely on. They would like to see more content of the same style every day.

As soon as you can ensure such consistency with each post, you will quickly grow your subscribers on Instagram in a short time.

Use Instagram Posts in Blog Posts

If you have a personal or business blog, you can include Instagram images in your posts. For example, if you work in the fashion industry, you can write an article on style tips on a blog. You can choose posts from Instagram, where you can show fashionable images of outfits. To do all this, go to the Instagram website on your desktop, go to your page, click on the message, click on the "..." icon, and click on "Embed." Then copy this link in the code section of your blog.

After a while, more and more people will visit your blog and will probably also view your Instagram account. It's rather a long-term game, especially if you don't get traffic. Adding posts to Instagram from the very beginning gives you greater visibility, and you will get huge profits in no time.

Watch out for your competitors

To get the desired number of subscribers on Instagram, you need to find people who follow the brands that you do, and are your competitors. Who are your main Instagram competitors in the current market? Keep a record of them and read their posts to see who comments on their posts. It will help you understand your preferences by following them and communicating with them.

Remember that it is better to choose small brands and competitors on Instagram. This is justified because if you sell makeup brushes and try to reach people with nail polish comments, there is a high probability that, despite the relevant niches, they are not the right audience. In particular, big brands tend to retain more customers. If you constantly follow other people who follow a competitor, you will undoubtedly get strong followers.

Appreciate your Followers on Instagram

One of the biggest mistakes people make when creating an account on Instagram is evaluating their subscribers as numbers. Subscribers are by no means the only indicator that matters to Instagram; however, you can focus on increasing the number of active subscribers, so that every person who joins you is actually a living and breathing person. Keep in mind that it does not matter what type of account you are using, whether it is a personal account or a business account.

Influencer

Another approach to increasing the number of subscribers on Instagram is to get noticed by influential individuals or to become an influence on influential individuals. An influential person already has loyal followers, and they can give you advice that will lead to the emergence of new subscribers for your account and, possibly, to some sales. Before hiring an influential person, be prepared to write a contract that prohibits the sender of fake traffic. Remember that the sudden appearance of followers in your account can lead to your account being blocked.

Hosting Giveaways

You can get more followers by posting on Instagram and having a small audience; however, if you post giveaways(?) on your website and use the option to track participants on Instagram, you have a much wider reach. If your audience is small, you can post your distribution to certain Facebook groups.

If you are just starting out, you can find more followers on Instagram; however, if you run such giveaways too often, you may not get the right audience. If your goal is to make sales, distributing free gifts does not necessarily help you attract more customers; however, this strategy can work well if you only want to quickly reach your Instagram subscribers.

Engage

Unlike other media such as television, magazines, newspapers, etc., Social networks allow you to add regular updates. Most Instagram users browse the app at least once a day and can discover if your company publishes new content. Depending on how the information you publish goes to your target audience, you can decide when and to what extent it should be published.

It is not only what you publish, the number of people you see, or the number with which they interact and share – the timing of your posts is crucial. Most B2B companies usually post messages during regular business hours. However, after a while you will notice that the posts posted during certain times of the day and certain days of the week receive better engagement than others.

Do your homework - know when your audience is likely to be online, and plan to post live when they are online.

Use Ideas

Insights can help you learn more about all the people who like your site, and who decides to follow you. As soon as you learn about the characteristics of your followers, you can adapt your posts to the needs of users and continue to interest them. For example, if a bookstore appeals to shoppers of all ages, but to most respondents between 18 and 25 years old, the offers they offer on Facebook must be designed according to the criteria of the type of audience they have. The offers they offer in the store should be more varied.

Use Geotags and Tags

The Instagram Geotag is similar to Facebook posting. Many people will post visible posts in their field. By tagging brands and large accounts, in addition to geo-tagging, you get the opportunity to become noticed by a large mass of subscribers.

There may be other ways to get more than

10,000 subscribers per month. You should not exclude them. Combine them with the ones discussed above to get more results.

Chapter 9: Instagram Sales Funnel

Without the appropriate marketing strategies, you cannot attract your target customers. No one will know anything about your business, what you offer, and exactly where your products are available. So, if you have not yet spent time and effort on this mission, now is the time to start. Obviously, getting started is easy with the sales funnel. This strategy got its name because this marketing strategy looks like a funnel on a chart.

Simply put, the sales funnel illustrates a perfect journey that can turn a potential customer into a paying one. Although you can sell your products or services to thousands of people, only a few provide contact information and become leaders. Only some of them become customers. Create your own Instagram sales funnel that produces results.

Instagram Ads

Instagram advertising has proven to be extremely useful for businesses and organizations of all types and sizes when it comes to marketing. Currently, advertising on Instagram is managed through the Facebook Ads Manager dashboard. This allows you to easily synchronize your paid services with Facebook and use different targeting options. If you can put it in a convenient place where you can profit from each transaction, you can scale the campaign by increasing your budget and achieving greater success.

Change your Bio to a Call-to-action

The Profile Bio is the main place where you are able to put down anything you want. You need to use the space to write only what your audience thinks is useful and what brings you and your brand closer. Using this section for a compelling call-to-action is one of the things you need to do when selling Instagram funnels. The application does not have enough space for text or links in the user interface. That is why you must be truly creative and make the most of your skills.

Use Custom Content

E-commerce products work very well when managed by user-generated content. This includes using other customers to promote your products to potential customers. This can be very useful for the practical implementation of the Instagram sales funnel. So, convince your subscribers to post photos of the product you are selling, tag your account, or use brand hashtags. If you attract powerful people, you have nailed it!

Custom content creates a culture that communicates your brand as a true consumer and contributes to its prominence. Using this tactic, you can create an online community focused on your business. This means that you have full customer support. By publishing photos generated by the user, viewers will be more inclined to attract others and encourage purchases if they do not own the product. Ultimately, you will develop constant interaction, increase your brand awareness, and turn most of your subscribers into buyers.

Join Influencers

With the right strategy, your brand can enter into a strategic partnership with a well-known, influential person. Make sure you get a high return on investment in terms of conversion and brand awareness. When you work with powerful people, you can use their network and brand to promote your e-commerce offerings. They will benefit from their success and popularity.

This method of spreading your marketing message is not similar to advertising, because the message comes from the personal and genuine voice of an influential person. Followers continue to greet Instagram supporters and influential supporters, despite the stricter restrictions on the transparency of sponsored content.

Link in Stories

This feature is only available for accounts with

more than 10,000 Instagram followers. This is another reason to prioritize on Instagram and attract an audience to take advantage of this feature. Users with such accounts can embed links in an Instagram story. Stories from Instagram are the main factor that gives companies more opportunities to implement their sales funnel.

Chapter 10: Increase Engagement on Instagram in 2019

In this section, you will learn about the different tips that you can follow to increase your engagement rate on Instagram.

Beat the New Algorithm

Instagram's new algorithm is designed such that it enables the creators to monetize this platform. At the end of the day, it is a business for them and they want to be profitable. If you are interested in engaging your audience, then you must post photos, upload videos, use Instagram Live, post Stories, reply to any comments or mentions you receive, you must also reply to the messages you get. If you are doing all this then you are on the right track. Now, comes the real question, how often do you do all this?

The greater is the time that you spend on Instagram and engage with your followers, the more Instagram will favor you. This implies that you have been doing the above-mentioned things regularly. In this section, you will learn about a couple of simple steps that you can follow to beat Instagram's algorithm.

Whenever you post something, then you must ensure that you are engaging with your followers within one hour of posting to increase your engagement. Your audience as well as Instagram will both appreciate it. In fact, Instagram will also boost your post and it will in turn increase your visibility online.

Whatever you do, please don't edit the caption on your post or the geotag for at least a day. If you do this, then it will reduce the chances of your post being seen by the desirable audience. Also, if you post something, please don't delete it to only repost it later. Doing these things will reduce the online visibility. If you delete something, then forget about it and don't ever post it again.

You can use up to 30 hashtags, but if you use 30

hashtags in every post, then such posts will be ticked off as spam by the algorithm. Instagram's algorithm will probably assume that you are spamming the other users and their feed. If this happens, then your reach will decline automatically. So, go through the chapter that discusses about using hashtags on Instagram in detail before you decide to use any. Also, if you repeatedly use the same set of hashtags in all your posts, then the algorithm will think that your account is a bot and will reduce your reach.

So, where can you post the hashtags? In the comments section or in the caption? Well, the answer to this question varies from one user to the next. Try posting in different sections and see which one works well for you. At times, the algorithm might think of the hashtags you post in the comments section as spam. So, try all this once and see the results for yourself.

If you geotag a popular destination, Instagram improves your reach. So, it is a good idea to visit all those places that are trending or are considered to be popular destinations and once there, post on your handle to increase your reach. Also, please don't tag a random photo off the web and tag it as a specific destination. Instagram has a recognition software and you cannot fool it.

Instagram keeps coming up with new features quite often. When you start using such features, then the same is noticed by Instagram as well and it will reward you for such behavior. You will be rewarded for simply using the new features- it will increase your visibility. So, whenever you notice that a new feature is released, please use it as soon as you can. By using these simple tips and the ones mentioned below, you can beat Instagram's algorithm.

How Often to Post?

If you want to attract more followers, then you need to increase your engagement rate and stay active, but how active must you be? Experts suggest that it is a good idea to post once or twice a day. It is not just about how many times you post; you must also know when to post. This is quintessential when you are dealing with Instagram's algorithm these days. There are some who suggest that you must post between 8 to 9 am while others suggest 2 to 5 pm for the first post. Some experts believe that 2 am is the ideal time to post for the second time. There is a lot of inconsistency regarding the ideal time to post, as the ideal time varies according to the expert that you want to follow.

Instead, an ideal way to go about this is to track the habits of your followers using the Insights on Instagram. This will help you identify the times when your followers are most active. According to this data, you can schedule your posts to ensure that the visibility of your posts increases. Also, if you post when your followers are active, then your posts will appear at the top of their feed. Find the ideal time to post, and post consistently.

Don't Preach

You must never try to preach and instead try to tell a story. Instagram is flooded with mediocre branding strategies that tend to forget that they are using a social media network that is supposed to be a platform for visual inspiration. You must try to captivate the attention of your audience using images and videos instead of preaching any marketing material. To increase your rate of engagement, it is quintessential that you become a visual storyteller. Provide them mini-stories through your captions, videos, pictures, and Instagram Stories. You can also try sharing any user-generated content that strikes a chord with your personal brand. If you are looking for some inspiration, then look at the profiles of brands that have turned into brilliant storytellers like Airbnb, Lego, Nike, and Red Bull.

Instagram Branding Matters

To increase your brand's awareness on Instagram, the three Cs are essential. The three Cs are creativity, clarity, and consistency. If your approach to Instagram is haphazard, then it simply will not work. There are certain core aspects that you must concentrate on, like the presentation of your profile, style patterns to keep your images fresh, and use of good hashtags. You must obviously keep interacting with your audience regularly to increase loyalty and engagement.

Explore Video Formats

A picture is certainly worth a thousand words, but a video is worth millions of views on Instagram. There are some who will vehemently deny this, but you cannot challenge the efficiency and the popularity of videos these days. Instagram recognizes this, and therefore it offers a variety of video options. From Stories made up of a combination of videos and stills into a single ad to 60-second videos – these are just two types of different video formats that Instagram offers to its users. For instance, you can use the live video option on Instagram Stories for any big reveals about a specific product or service. You can also use this to post any prerecorded ads or behind-the-scenes footage to engage your audience and increase their interest in the content that you post.

Video Subtitles

Videos are certainly dominating the online domain these days, and audio has become the poor cousin because a majority of users don't usually enable sound when viewing a video. That's why it is important that you start using subtitles to show that you are able to drive the message home through a video even when the audio is disabled. Use subtitles to increase the rate of engagement. If the viewer can see the message you are trying to convey, it increases their interest and might even prompt them to respond to the Stories or videos you post.

Video Ad Formats

A majority of Instagram users tend to take a specific action like visiting a site, searching for something or even telling a friend after a post influences them. So, it is quintessential that you try to master a wide range of ad formats that are offered by this platform. Photo ads are certainly quite popular, but Instagram has introduced video formats that are a great tool to target your selected audience.

There are three formats to create ads on Instagram: single video ads, carousels, and Instagram Stories. The single video ads provide an opportunity to design an ad for up to 60 seconds. The carousel feature enables you to add more than one still to the video so that the user can keep swiping to explore more videos or images. Instagram Stories provides a full-screen format where the images and videos can be mixed together to create ads that are visually engaging.

Don't Forget about GIFs

A lot of people tend to only watch entire videos that are less than 15 seconds. So, being able to create and post a GIF is an essential skill for anyone who dreams of making it big on

Instagram. The GIF format certainly holds more appeal than a picture. GIFs are usually more shared than images in JPEG or PNG formats. Additionally, GIFs are certainly more cost-effective than producing a video. This has certainly inspired Instagram as well to create their own version of a GIF - the Boomerang feature – a feature that enables the user to record a short video of stills before seamlessly combining them and looping them in a format that goes backward and forward. Instagram does it all; you merely need to record the video and then it is ready to be uploaded. This tool has certainly produced wonderful results and is a great way to catch the viewer's attention. The Boomerang craze doesn't look like it will be slowing down any time soon.

The Right Hashtags

When it comes to Instagram posts, being able to select the right hashtags can make all the difference in the visibility of your posts. The right hashtags will ensure that your posts stay on top, whereas the wrong ones will sink your post to the bottom where they will be soon forgotten. If you make your hashtags generic, then your posts will need to face tough competition from millions of other posts. Instead, the perfect hashtag strategy recommends that the hashtags you use must be a mixture of popular and niche-specific hashtags. Doing this will help you connect with your target audience.

Another thing that matters when you are using hashtags is the number of hashtags you use. You can use up to 30 hashtags per post on Instagram under your caption. If you use 30 hashtags on every post, then it will make your posts seem unprofessional and even untargeted. Most of the top brands limit their hashtag usage to less than ten. The right number of hashtags for you will depend on the niche you are operating in and the way your competitors are using hashtags. You will need to experiment a couple of times before you can find the sweet spot. You will learn more about choosing hashtags in the coming chapters.

Direct Instagram Traffic to Increase Website Traffic

You can use your Instagram traffic to increase the website visits by including a clickable link in your bio. Try to make the most of this opportunity. To do this, you can promote your link with offers and promotions to prompt the visitors to click through on the link. You must also include certain strong calls-to-action with your URL. All the ad formats on Instagram offer a CTA button that directs the visitor to a specific landing page or website. If you are collaborating with an influencer, then you can ask them to promote your URL in the content that they post. To ensure that you have the necessary traffic statistics with you, you should use an analytics tool to check the content that drives traffic to your website.

Using SEO

Instagram and SEO might seem like strange bedfellows but developing an SEO strategy for your profile is critical while competing on this platform. The two important areas that influence SEO are your account name and your handle. The account handle is the "@" name that you register on Instagram, and it must clearly show the niche in which you operate. Please keep in mind that Instagram can identify the content you post. If something that doesn't gel with your handle, then don't expect to see your posts in the Explore section. The account name is the name that is visible under your profile picture on Instagram, and it must reflect your account handle and the niche. Whenever someone searches any words or emojis on Instagram, then it is your account name that Instagram will check for to provide them suitable results.

Filters and Third-Party Applications

The wide array of filters and third-party apps available these days are certainly helpful. Since Instagram is a platform that's predominantly designed for visual media, one of the most popular features is the filter option it offers. You can use different filters to make your posts more attractive and eye-catching. If you use certain filters consistently, then it will help generate a unique identity for your personal brand. According to a social media report published by WebDam, a majority of the top brands tend to use the same set of filters whenever they post. Apart from the inbuilt filters, you also have numerous third-party apps you can use. You have the option of choosing from an extensive selection of photo editing apps to apps that help create captions and everything else in between.

Another thing that you can do is pair up with an influencer. You will learn more about this in the coming chapters.

Chapter 11: Selecting Hashtags on Instagram

If you look at the Instagram profile of any influencer, then you will notice that they are always well-curated. It is more than just beautiful clothes and aesthetically arranged tabletops that entice followers. One of the important ways in which you can draw in the right audience is by using the right hashtags on Instagram. So, how can you find the best hashtags on Instagram? The good news is that brands and businesses alike are fine-tuning their hashtag strategies over the years. When it comes to hashtags on Instagram, there is much more to it than what meets the eye. In this section, you will learn about the different things that you must keep in mind while selecting a hashtag and they are as follows.

Weeding out Dead Tags

The first thing that you must do is always get rid of any dead tags and keep revamping your strategy every couple of months. The best way to search for hashtags is by identifying the leaders in your niche and checking their profiles to find the hashtags that they use. Make a list of all those hashtags and spend some time checking those hashtags. If you notice that many are using a certain hashtag to post content related to your niche, then you have just stumbled across a hot hashtag. If the hashtag has over 10,000 but less than 1 million users, then it is great! Anything under 10,000 isn't that popular yet, and if the number exceeds 1 million, it means that the hashtag has saturated or has even turned into spam. Ensure that those who have been using that hashtag have been doing so recently. If it hasn't been used for a couple of weeks now, then it means that you have a dead hashtag at hand.

Look at all the top posts for the chosen hashtag. If there is an account with a good following or content, then look at what other hashtags are used in the account and repeat this process. Keep doing this until you have at least 60-90 hashtags handy. You can use these hashtags in rotation to see what works best for you and generates the best engagement rate. I suggest that it is a good idea to revamp your hashtag research every four months or do it as soon as you notice a decrease in your engagement. A common mistake that a lot of users make while using hashtags is that they use irrelevant hashtags, dead hashtags, or use hashtags when their profile is on private!

Balance is Essential

You must try to balance the hashtags that you use. On Instagram, you can use up to 30 hashtags for a post. So, an ideal strategy is to use the top ten popular hashtags from your niche and industry and then use another 10-20 specific and niche hashtags with the low-medium rate of competition in a post. A simple way to do this is by typing in a keyword you want to use in the search bar of Instagram. You can also check what the other hashtag pages within your niche or industry are posting and select the ones that you like.

You will need to tweak your hashtag strategy to make room for improvement constantly. Try to use quite popular and broad Instagram hashtags like #business, #fashion or #food along with other niche tags.

Think About Your Audience

You can use hashtags to increase your Instagram presence effectively, but there are various misconceptions about hashtags and the ways in which you can use them. The two common mistakes that lots of users make is using too few hashtags or using only the extremely popular ones. Keep in mind that you can use up to 30 hashtags. For instance, if you use a popular hashtag like #fun, then you are competing with over 300 million other posts with the same hashtag. If there are a lot of users using the same hashtag, then the chances of your post being seen will certainly be reduced. You must try to use hashtags that don't have more than 200,000 posts attached to it. It helps to increase the visibility of your posts under the "recent" category and increase your exposure.

When you start looking for ideal hashtags, start by making a list of hashtags that your target audience is probably looking for. The next step is to search for that hashtag on Instagram and check the list that shows up. Go through the top posts and see if there are any similarities to your content. Once you view a hashtag on Instagram, it will show you several other related hashtags as well. These hashtags can be quite good, and you can add them to your list.

Keep in mind that you must not only create content that's appealing to your audience, but you must also ensure that your content is visible to your audience. The best way to do this is by using relevant hashtags.

Don't Hashtag Every Word of The Caption

Users tend to go overboard when it comes to using hashtags. It certainly doesn't make any sense to use hashtags for every word in your caption. Try to limit yourself to about two or three keywords in your caption and find relevant hashtags only for those words. If you hashtag all the words in the caption, then you will hurt the visibility of your posts.

Chapter 12: Instagram Influencers

So, what is an influencer? An influencer is someone with the power to sway others' decisions. In this case, I am talking about the power of social media. In a world of social media frenzy, brands realize the value of an Instagram account because it helps them increase their market reach. The reach of an account is based on the number of people who follow it and the number of people who actively engage with the said profile by liking and commenting on posts. With the new Instagram algorithm, rate of engagement has become quite important. Brands are eager to see an active user base. This is something that no one can fake, and it cannot be purchased. So, the rate of engagement is the real criteria to determine the market reach.

If you are reading this book, then you are somewhat keen on going down this path. Maybe you want to create your Instagram account and are wondering what all of this is about. Maybe you have already taken the first steps and are now wondering whether it will be worth your while or not.

The first question that you might have in your mind is about the required size of your Instagram account before you can start working with brands. You don't necessarily need a massive follower base to start working with brands. The new Instagram algorithm has brought about an interesting and favorable change by leveling the playing field. In the past, small accounts on Instagram weren't capable of competing with the large and well-established ones. For instance, in the past, you might have never seen a lesser-known account that is listed on the explore section; however, the new algorithm is designed in such a way that it rewards the rate of engagement and therefore helps even the smallest accounts. This is the reason why on the explore page, along with the top 9 list of hashtags, you will come across photos that have

4000 likes and another one with just 300 likes that are both listed side by side under the heading "top posts." They are determined based on the percentage of engagement instead of the number of followers. This goes on to show how much Instagram values engagement these days.

So, when is the ideal time to start collaborating with brands? Well, this decision is entirely up to you; however, it is a good idea to start collaborating with brands once you have the following things in place:

- Your account has more than 1000 followers (this is merely a guideline, but it shows that you are building your account).

- Your account has a consistent track record of at least six months. Before that, you must concentrate on creating and developing your feed. If you start collaborating too early, then it will divert your interest from creating valuable content.

- You have a couple of small businesses that have already approached you in the past.

- Your posts are gaining recognition, and your posts tend to appear under the "top post" category.

It is quite obvious that all this will look different for different users since each account has a specific pace at which it grows. Every account is also unique according to the individual who creates it. If you happen to be a skilled photographer, then it will certainly give you an edge over the others in your field; however, if you are just getting started with photography, then it will take your posts longer to gain some recognition. If you have a professional degree or a certificate saying you specialize in something, it is certainly an advantage for you over the others in your niche. If you commit yourself to your account, work hard, and spend some time posting valuable, creative and authentic content, then the learning curve on IG will be shorter, and your feed will grow faster than someone who doesn't do these things.

So, can you approach a brand? Yes, you can approach a brand as soon as your account meets the above-mentioned criteria. You might be waiting for a brand to approach you, but don't do that. Remember that you must always be proactive in life if you want something. You cannot keep waiting for an opportunity to come knocking at your door. Instead, make the first move and seek them out!

If you find a brand, business, or company that you think will be a good fit for your account, don't hesitate to approach them. You must remember that there are tens of thousands of influencers on Instagram today and if you want to stand out, then you need to take the first step. You can approach a brand and tell them that you are genuinely interested in what they do and that you think about collaborating with you will be helpful for all the parties involved. While doing this, prepare yourself for any potential rejections.

Even if they are interested in your offer, they can put you on the backburner and might not want to start working immediately.

What will any early collaboration look like? Usually, most of the early collaborations you can expect will be with small businesses with little or even no marketing budget. When you think about it, this makes sense. Why will a business want to work with someone who doesn't have a great market reach yet? They will want to do this because of their budgets involved, and that's perfectly acceptable. All of this will help you gain experience, and it will prove to be invaluable later on. Early collaborations are quite important. This is an opportunity for you to show the world and all the potential collaborators your style of photography, your marketing tactics, and your creativity. Usually, an early Instagram collaboration will have the following characteristics:

- It is usually for just products.

- The offer is from a small business or a growing company.

- The collaboration requirements are quite simple. – They may offer to give you a sample of their product in exchange for a post or a feature in your story.

- A written contract might or might not exist.

- It is often intimate and personal.

- It enables you to do the necessary groundwork for any future collaboration with the same business.

- It is an opportunity for you to showcase your skills.

Here are the list of pros and cons you must keep in mind if you are working with a product company.

It is a chance for you to receive some "free" products that you might enjoy. You might receive some items that seem luxurious, but you might not want to spend your money on. The products might be quite useful and add value to your life. You will certainly be able to produce content for your Instagram feed. It is a chance to nurture a mutually beneficial relationship with the business or brand. You can generate a good track record for yourself by demonstrating your skills.

On the downside, chances are that you will receive products that you don't necessarily need or like. All the products can start to pile up. You might have to pay some taxes or duties on the products you receive, so they aren't entirely "free." Also, businesses tend to think that they can pay you in products instead of giving you a proper payment.

Since you are just getting started with collaborating, working with product companies is as good a place as any to get started. It is a critical aspect of your training period. Also, if you do it well, it is beneficial for all the parties involved. As you start to gain some steam as an influencer, you can slowly start to ask for compensation that is not in the form of products or other freebies.

When it comes to Instagram collaborations, here are a couple of general rules that you must keep in mind regardless of the complexity or the nature of the collaboration.

You must always take some time out and carefully understand all the requirements before agreeing to do anything. To avoid any confusion or ambiguity, it is a good idea to get everything in writing. For instance, if you get started with your collaboration and then receive a list of instructions or requirements that you were previously unaware of, it puts you in a precarious position. There are two outcomes of such a situation: you will either end up doing extra work, or you will end up refusing the offer, and it will certainly ruin any chances of future collaboration with them. If you want to do a good job and make everyone happy, then you must be aware of what you are expected to do. Even if the collaboration offer you receive isn't desirable, don't be rude; always be polite and professional. You must be professional whilst doing your work. It means that you must adhere to deadlines and respond promptly.

So, how do you decide who to collaborate with? Before you decide to collaborate with anyone, keep a simple thing in mind - every post of yours has the potential to either help or hurt your feed. While collaborating with someone, you tend to put in your integrity, authenticity, and trust. It might sound simple, but these things are very important if you want to make it big on Instagram. Go with your gut and carefully consider all things before agreeing to something. A lucrative contract can be quite tempting to accept, but if you lose your followers' trust in this process, it isn't worth it.

Here are some factors that you must consider while thinking about any collaboration:

Is the company, business or the product you want

to collaborate with in sync with your niche, interests, style, and will they complement your profile? You must never underestimate the importance of this step. If it is in sync, then it is favorable for you, your followers, as well as the business. If it isn't, then your posts will seem out of place, and it will come across as merely an advertisement. All of this will hurt your following, and it won't do the business any good either.

What are the costs involved? You must carefully consider the time and work that is required for the collaboration. When it comes to Instagram influencing, time is essentially money. You must have a rough estimate of the time, effort, and any other costs that are involved. Consider the actual benefits you stand to gain. Yes, exposure is a great thing, but does it pay your bills in the end? While you are weighing in the benefits, also consider any potential benefits you stand to gain. At times, an early Instagram collaboration paves the way for future collaborations, and that's a good incentive to work with. Don't take up any work that you know you will not be able to complete on time or in a proper manner. If you overextend yourself, then your quality of work will suffer.

How much can you start charging for collaboration or a post? This topic is certainly the elephant in the room, and it is time that we address it. This is one aspect of collaborating that frustrates a lot of people. There is no specific answer to this question, and you must decide the price you want to work for and the time spent on a project. The answer usually depends on the time that's available to you, the number of jobs you have on hand, how worthy it is to you and such. The usual going rate for an Instagram post is around $5-$10 per 1000 followers. So, if your account has 100,000 followers, then you can charge anywhere between $500-$1000 per post. There might be times when you are negotiating, and a business might agree to pay a portion of the payment in kind. It is entirely up to you whether you want to take their offer or not.

What about collaborating for free? Again, this is your decision. If you are just getting started, then I suggest that you accept a project free of cost. Doing this is a great way to display your skills to the world. Also, if you do a good job, you can gain better opportunities in the future. Apart from this, it will all prove to be a valuable learning experience. Exposure is quintessential when you are getting started, and it sets the tone for your future projects or collaborations.

Negotiating is another important aspect of collaboration. In fact, it is a terribly underrated skill. Negotiating is about coming to a mutually beneficial compromise. Take a moment and ask yourself how keen you are on working with this business. If you are keen to work with them, then coming to a compromise will be quite easy. If your gut says otherwise, then politely decline the offer and walk away. You can bend as much as you want. You must know yourself, your brand, and understand whether the offer is a favorable one for you or not. Time and effort are scarce resources, and you must choose carefully.

While negotiating, you must never make the first move by throwing out numbers. Instead, always ask for their budget. Have a couple of numbers ready in mind and offer at least two options for negotiation. Always keep your emotions in check and respond logically. Be willing to listen and stay positive.

I believe that every collaboration is quite unique. As you start to travel down this path, you will learn a lot. Along the way, you will be able to determine your priorities as well as your parameters. Keep the following things in mind before you decide to collaborate with anyone:

- Do you love what the business does or what their brand represents?

- Do you have sufficient time for collaboration?

- Does the business or brand fall in line with

the image you are trying to build or maintain?

- Do you want to build the base for any future collaboration with the said business?

- Is there any scope for any collaboration in the future?

- Will this collaboration help your feed?

- Will your followers accept this product, or will it hurt your integrity?

- What are the different costs involved?

- How will you benefit from it and do the benefits outweigh any costs?

Collaborations on Instagram offer plenty of opportunities; however, you will be able to come out on top only when you know how to navigate. Test the waters before you take the plunge. You will learn more about this in the coming chapters.

Chapter 13: Collaboration Ideas

Collaboration on Instagram doesn't necessarily have to be with brands. You can also collaborate with other Instagrammers to increase your reach. In this section, you will learn about different ideas for effective and efficient collaboration.

Taking Over Each Other's Pages

The first idea of collaboration is taking over each other's pages on Instagram. This might sound scary, but it is quite effective. When you swap the controls of your respective pages, you will be able to provide a new flavor or twist to the posts and also increase the scope of interactions with your followers. You can do all this quite easily. If you manage to execute it properly and ensure that the content stays entertaining, then very few will have a negative reaction to it. It is a good idea not to extend this for more than a week at most. Ideally, stick to a day or a couple of days but nothing more than that. If you do this for too long, you will alienate your audience, and all your effort will not add up to anything in the end.

Guest Appearance

Another great way in which you can collaborate with other Instagrammers is by making an appearance in each other's posts or photographs. All you need to do is tag the other person you are collaborating with. Also, it is a great way to generate organic interest in each other's profiles, and it encourages the followers or audience to check the other person's profile on their own time. You don't have to ask them to do anything; you just have to tag the other person and let your audience feel like they are looking at the other profile on their own accord without any suggestion from you. This is an effective way of ensuring a successful crossover on Instagram.

Making a Video Together

Make a video together and post it on both your profiles. You must provide a direct link to the other person's Instagram profile while doing this to ensure that the audience of both the pages see it and it automatically encourages the viewers to view the other person's profile without any prompting. You can post a short video within the time restriction suggested by the platform. Search for some creative ideas for this video. As long as you ensure that the video is of good quality and is engaging and entertaining, you will be able to engage your audience. While collaborating for videos, ensure that you don't collaborate with more than two or three people at once. If you exceed this number, then you will end up overwhelming your audience, and they will quickly lose interest.

Start a Challenge

This is a brilliant idea. Starting a challenge post is quite easy, and it is easy to spread. In fact, the trend will catch up quickly because it encourages people to engage in interactive activities and pass on the challenge to their friends. You can come up with a challenge idea together and then post the related posts on both your profiles. You need to come up with a special hashtag for the challenge to ensure that it is captivating. If your challenge is entertaining and you do all that's necessary, then it will make others curious about what the buzz is all about. You must spell out the rules and restrictions for the challenge in an original post and then wait for social media to work its magic. The challenge will work quite well if you provide an incentive. So, the person who does it best will stand to win something, and it acts as a good motivator. You don't necessarily have to do this, but it is an option available.

Contests

This is quite similar to the previous idea. According to the execution of the idea, it works just like a challenge. Running a contest will help you test the limits to which your audience is willing to go. With a challenge post, you will need something that's reasonable enough that people will attempt it within an hour or two; however, with a contest, you can truly go wild because you will be offering a prize. The better the prize is, the more exciting it will be. For someone to participate in the contest, they will need to share the original post and use the contest-specific hashtag you created. The idea of winning a prize is a great incentive, and it will motivate the users to do something on their own accord.

Running a Loop Giveaway

For a loop giveaway, you will either require multiple people or a loop. In this, entrants will be asked to follow a loop and follow all those who are a part of the loop to win a prize. Typically, you will do this by asking everyone to post the same photograph, then tag another person in the chain, so all that the participant needs to do is keep clicking and following the other profiles to enter the giveaway. Because of all the effort that's involved, the prize in this giveaway must be good enough to make it appealing.

Start a Page

This is quite simple, but a lot of people don't seem to think about it. A great way to collaborate is by starting a page together. This page doesn't necessarily include any personal posts, instead, you can select a theme and post content related to that theme. You can post pictures, memes, or anything else that goes with the theme you select. If your collaboration page is popular, then you both will receive new followers to your main accounts from the page that you are running together.

Working Together on Sponsorships

You can collaborate with other Instagrammers to work together on sponsored posts. A lot of Instagrammers work with sponsors so this is a two-sided relationship where the Instagrammer works for an incentive, and the sponsor will receive their due advertising. If you work with another Instagrammer, then you can make the sponsorship deal more lucrative for the brand.

You can use any or all of the ideas given in this chapter to start collaborating on Instagram. If you have any other ideas, now is the time to test them! Instagram is a platform to display your creativity to the world, so make the most of it.

Chapter 14: Become an Instagram Influencer

There are a lot of brands that spend a lot of money to leverage influencer marketing. The marketing budgets go into tens of thousands of dollars. If you aren't sure of how you can use your Instagram account to become an influencer and generate money from it, don't worry, because you will learn about it in this section. Here are the steps that you can follow:

Defining your Niche

Instagram boasts of over 800 million active monthly users. If you want to become an influencer, then your aim must be to stand out. You need to appeal to a specific audience and select a topic so that you can build around it. Times have certainly changed - to start a profitable business you don't need a fancy website. In fact, all that you need is a good Instagram account. If you aren't certain what niche to select, here are the five most profitable niches on Instagram today.

Health and Fitness

Do you want to show off your workout routine to the rest of the world? Are you interested in promoting a healthy way of living? Are you passionate about anything related to health and fitness? Do you want to inspire others with your healthy recipes? If yes, then you can select this niche. You might think that this is an oversaturated niche and that there is no space left for any newbies. Please don't let this hype fool you. If you are good at something, then there will always be a spot open for you. A brilliant thing about highly competitive niches is that even if you manage to get a tiny slice of such a niche it will be quite substantial. In fact, fitness and health is an evergreen niche. People will always be curious and interested in learning about different diets, recipes, and workout regimes that will help them achieve their fitness and health goals. Staying fit and healthy never goes out of fashion and if you have a knack for it, then go ahead and take the leap.

Beauty

Do you get extremely excited whenever someone comes up with a new cosmetic product line? Does the thought of Rihanna's 'Fenty' or Kylie Jenner's cosmetics make your heart skip a beat? Do your friends constantly ask you to help them with their makeup or hair? Do others constantly ask you about your beauty secrets? Do you spend hours together trying out the new beauty hacks that you see online? A simple way in which makeup artists, as well as hairstylists, make a lot of money is by reviewing products online and by sharing tips or making tutorials. If you have a flair for it, then hop aboard the Instagram beauty train! The key to being successful in a competitive niche like this is through self-expression. You must be able to think outside the box and find some fresh ways in which you can leverage your expertise to increase your bank balance. Maybe you have some great hacks to deal with skin problems and you know they work

- share that valuable information. Maybe you are good at recreating looks straight off the runway on a very low budget - don't hold back. You can get as creative as you want. If you manage to stand apart from all the beauty influencers on Instagram, then you can perhaps gain the attention of your favorite brands too!

Travel

Do you like to explore new places? Does the term "wanderlust" strike a chord with you? How does the idea of living your life out of a suitcase sound to you? Do others often ask you "where are you?" instead of "how are you?" If traveling is something that you love, then this is the niche for you! In fact, in 2017, one of the highest searched phrases was "how to become a travel blogger." However, not everyone is interested in starting a full-time travel blog. Good news is that you don't really need a blog to satisfy your wanderlust. All that you need to do is pick the right travel niche. Here are a couple of examples of a sub-niche in travel: backpacking, luxury, family vacations, traveling tips for a specific demographic (college students, millennials...etc.), or a specific form of travel (single-female traveler, adventure junkie, or leisure travel). The more specific your niche is, the greater your chances are of making it big.

Business

Do you have a successful business? Do you have plenty of knowledge about how businesses work? Do you think you can help others in their business endeavors? Are you good at teaching others and are you passionate about it? Regardless of how the market is doing, people are always looking for ways in which they can maximize their wealth. You don't necessarily need a Fortune 500 company to become a business influencer. All you need is to have sufficient knowledge to teach others to achieve their goals. Maybe you consider yourself a tech guru, or you have some brilliant tips that can help people generate traffic from different sources. As long as you think you have the necessary information to help others achieve their business goals, you can get started.

Fashion

Another evergreen niche is fashion. Are you passionate about fashion? Are you always updated about the recent fashion trends? Do others look up to you for fashion advice? Does it make your heart tingle to think about attending New York Fashion Week? To become a successful influencer in this niche, you must ask yourself what the one thing that sets you apart from all others in this niche is. Maybe you can concentrate on environmentally-conscious brands, or you are probably good at giving DIY advice or fashion hacks. Perhaps you can give advice about how people can recreate high-end looks on a low budget? Well, the good news is that there is no mold that you must fit into to become a fashion influencer.

If you can dominate a niche, it doesn't matter whether you have 4,000 or 40,000 followers. It helps you create an audience base that is highly engaged. This enables you to foster trust with your followers.

High-Quality Posts

This certainly sounds simple, but the reality is quite different. The quality of the content that you post will determine your number of followers as well as their rate of engagement. You certainly cannot expect to attract tons of followers by posting blurry selfies or dimly lit, unfocused pictures; however, if you share high-quality pictures or images (aesthetically pleasing pictures that aren't pixelated) that are inspiring, educating, and entertaining, you are headed in the right direction.

If you want to see your account grow, then you must invest in a smartphone with a good camera or a DSLR and spend some time taking pictures that have good lighting, are well focused, and have a good composition. Don't be under the impression that your work ends here. You must also ensure that you come up with engaging captions and use the appropriate hashtags to attract your ideal audience.

A Single Design Theme

Having a constant aesthetic is one feature that differentiates the accounts of influencers from that of regular Instagrammers. When you have a cohesive feed, it helps your audience understand what they can expect by following your account. In fact, if you have a single design theme for your feed, it increases the rate of engagement by keeping the viewers interested and compels them to spend more time on your profile. If you want to work or collaborate with brands, then the one metric that plays a significant role in this process is your engagement stats. You must find a feed design that is sync with the topic or niche you opt for.

Consistent Posting Schedule

The new algorithm of Instagram rewards all the users who post consistently. Why is this? The reason is quite obvious - Instagram wants users, and the reward is that it pushes up popular accounts in the feed. You might want to post daily, thrice a day or even just once a week. Regardless of when you want to post, try to stick to a consistent schedule. There are certain tools like Later or Planoly that help you plan your feed for the week. It merely takes an hour or two to curate the content you want to post, along with the captions and the hashtags you want to use. If you are consistent in the way you post, then it will make your audience check your profile like clockwork.

Engage

If you look at the Instagram profiles of any of the most popular influencers, then you will notice that they don't merely post a picture and log out of their account. They usually insert a question in their captions, spend some time responding to the comments and DMs, and engage with other accounts. Doing this helps establish a strong sense of community around your personal brand and turns all those casual swipers into a loyal audience.

To increase engagement with your audience, you can do something as simple as posting a poll in one of your Instagram stories. You can also ask them for their opinions on different things that you might want to do. Engaging with your audience is similar to striking up a conversation in person. A great way to understand what your audience likes while strengthening your relationship with them is by asking for their feedback.

Collaborating

Have you ever come across the saying, "It isn't about what you know, but who you know?" Well, this couldn't be any truer for Instagram. You can certainly grow your account on your own, but when you collaborate with others, it certainly speeds up this process. It also helps you network with others in your niche and will make you privy to those opportunities that you were previously unaware of. So, take some time and go through the popular hashtags in your niche and identify similar accounts. Go through their content, strike up a conversation, and then see how that goes. It might present an opportunity for collaboration in the future.

Reach Out to Brands

Once you have over 1000 followers, it is time to start reaching out to the brands within your chosen niche. Even if you are a small account, it is okay to start pitching. If you have a good rate of engagement and your audience is similar to the brand's ideal audience, then there is a good chance that you can collaborate with such brands. Create the perfect pitch and come up with a detailed offer of what the brand stands to gain by associating themselves with you. You might feel awkward initially, but it gets easier with practice. After all, what is the worst that can happen to you? They might reject your offer, and that's about it. You don't stand to lose anything, and you can gain a lot if it goes well.

Chapter 15: Social Media Principles

Use only platforms that are suitable for your business

The fact that you want to include social media in your business-marketing plan does not mean that you have to use all available platforms. You would need too much time to study each and then implement a plan. No one, even the most experienced marketer, can handle more than a few accounts at the same time. See what they have to offer and decide if they are suitable for promoting your business. Twitter and Facebook can have the most subscribers; however, this does not mean that they have the right amount of your target audience. The best choice could be one of the smaller platforms.

Data matters

There is only one way to determine if your efforts are working effectively, and that is to evaluate all the data. Some social networking platforms have built-in tools to help you, and there are many third-party analytics tools. Use them to see which answers are most relevant to the content that you share or advertise, and most importantly, which ones do not correspond to the required response level. That way you can figure out what to quit and what to do next.

Create your connections

One of the most common mistakes that social media marketers make is talking to their audience, not with them. Talk to your subscribers and chat with them, they want to know that you are a person and not just a computer that runs automatic answers. Ask them to share their thoughts and make sure that you respond to their comments promptly. When they send you messages, immediately communicate with them. If you effectively ignore potential customers, they will simply be crowded out.

Go visual

Large blocks of text shun people away, but they stop to view pictures. Photos, videos, and infographics contain information that makes it easier for people to write. Make sure your visual content is strong, attractive, and relevant to your business.

Make each of your chosen platforms unique

There are many tools to share content across multiple platforms. People who follow you on a platform are likely to follow you on all of them and do not want to see identical content. Make each of your accounts unique, as it will attract more people and will get you more followers and more potential customers.

Make people follow you

If someone is following you on a social network, they are likely to want some recognition for it. Offer a premium for a subscription - perhaps a small discount on a product or participation in a random draw. People need an incentive to join you, and you will attract and interest them if you do any of this.

Be a "personable" person

While social networks are a more relaxed way to promote your business, you still need to be professional. Provide personal information that will give your business a human face, such as a birthday or a joke, but never share personal views on things on your business page. If you start talking too much about politics or certain celebrities, you can easily turn your followers away from you.

If it doesn't work, change tactics

Not everything will work. No matter how much analysis you conduct or how many new team members you have hired, there will be a platform that is simply not suitable for your business. If nothing works and you get no results from it, drop it and leave. There are better things for your time and energy to be used on.

Build relationships with companies

If there are companies in the same industry as you, connect with them and follow them, but only if this is not direct competition. You can get linked to customers, share subscribers, and get tips. Maybe it will surprise you how many good things come out of it, so try it, but don't follow either one account indiscriminately - be picky.

Fight trolls

The more successful you become, the more attention your social network accounts attract, and that means the inevitable insults of some people. If you find haters on your pages, be professional in dealing with them. Choose carefully how you should respond - sometimes it must be a polite response, in other cases, it is better to ignore it, and in some cases, you will have to block the user. Do not block anyone just because they do not like your company. It does not make sense for business, and it does not send good news.

Don't try to sell

Your main goal is to sell, and that is why you are in business, but when it comes to social networks, it is a great sin. People who follow you do not want to constantly view advertising material. They are not to do you a favor; they want to have fun and learn. They want to build relationships and seek entertainment. If they want to purchase a product, they will directly look for you, whether on social networks, on your website, or through other means.

Complete your business profile

There is enough space in your profile to provide your subscribers with information about you. If you leave parts of it empty, you will not engage your subscribers. They want to know everything about yourself; they want to know what it costs to be watched and supported. Spaces indicate that you are not interested, and no one will take the time to subscribe to someone who cannot fill out their profile.

Make social media your plan

Think of it as another area of your business. It must be goal-oriented, and you need goals that are included in your business plan. This allows you to measure how valuable social media is for your overall plan.

Get your audience hooked

The ultimate goal of any marketing plan is to get people to read your content. You want these people to hang onto every word you write to see what comes next. You want them to check if you publish something constantly. The only way to do this is to provide high-quality, valuable, and relevant content.

Make it easy to share your content

Although the technological age has allowed us to do as little as possible, if you want to share your content, you need to put in work. You need to present your content in such a way that it is easy to share and provide users with the buttons necessary to send content to a friend or another individual from their social networking pages. Make it harder for them not to do it.

If you share something, comment on it

Do not just click a button that allows you to share or send something. Add a comment to let people know why you think content is worth sharing. This will help you create your own know-how and declare yourself as an expert. This in itself increases the value of everything you share.

Check your grammar and spelling

Grammar and spelling are important. You are a professional, and the worst thing you can do is publish content that is poorly written and contains spelling errors. Review your work, review it again, and double-check to make sure it is written professionally before publishing it.

The engagement pattern of your followers

Make sure that you are posting actively on Instagram according to the engagement pattern of your followers. When it seems that they are most likely to engage, that's when you should post. This will take a while to get it right, and spend some time trying to figure this out. It might not sound important, but it most certainly is. You will realize this only when your followers and the number of "likes" your posts receive will grow.

Do not post collages

A picture is worth a thousand words. A collage of 44 images, however, is not worth 44,000 words. If you want to promote your brand or business on Instagram successfully, make sure that the images you post are clear, recognizable, and large. Keep things simple.

Tags are important

Tags are very important. Yes, certain people exaggerate tagging; however, tags help users identify their content. Be prudent while using tags.

Do not post screenshots

Use high quality and high-resolution photos for your Instagram posts. Assess the quality and clarity of the image before posting to Instagram. Often Instagram does not support screenshots made on mobile phones.

Don't ask for likes

It's pretty silly that people tend to ask others to like your posts or follow your page on Instagram. Please do not do this. If the user likes something, he genuinely "likes" the post. You should not ask him. These similar requests can repel people, and not attract them. You certainly don't want this, right?

Chat with people who share your content

If someone publishes a link to your latest content or replies to a message, take the time to thank him. These are the people you want to have on your page, people who generate a lot of free advertising for you. Build a good relationship with them and encourage them to share your content.

Learn the platform guidelines

Familiarize yourself with the policies of each platform and make sure you know what is acceptable regarding behavior and content. Common sense should dictate that you like the content and should check the conditions for the platform before publishing it. Some platforms, especially Facebook, are constantly changing their rules, such as rules regarding running competitions, and if they are broken, can lead to a fine, suspension, or a complete ban from the platform.

Make sure your profile contains your location

People need to know where your business is located, even if your service or product is online, so they can access you. If they know where you are, they can find you and check your business out, especially on Facebook. This is more important if you have a physical store that people can visit. If you do not add your location, you may lose a lot of potential customers.

Strategic Bio

The bio that you can use on LinkedIn or even Facebook is not like the one that you can use on Instagram. As I have already mentioned, there is a limit prescribed on the number of characters you can use in the bio so you must use it strategically. No one is really interested about your various qualifications or anything like that on Instagram. The Instagram bio is not your resume and you must not make it seem like one. This is your chance to make yourself seem interesting so that all those who view your profile are eager to start following you. You need a bio that will humanize your brand. You need to convey your primary objective in a simple way that appeals to your target audience. Also, the bio gives the viewer a general idea of the things that they can expect from your profile.

Utilize all social media platforms

Most marketers believe that a far-reaching marketing campaign is impossible without the use of various available social networks. This may be right, but not necessary. The social networking platforms you choose should fit your audience. It makes no sense to develop a brilliant marketing strategy for the platform if your target audience is not even active on there. The various social networking platforms you use will also depend on your audience, budget, and campaign. If you have time and budget constraints, it is recommended to focus on one or two platforms, rather than all platforms. If you are trying to use more than two platforms at the same time, it is very likely that the content you create will not be personalized for each platform. It's simple: if your audience does not use Twitter, you do not need a campaign for Twitter. You cannot spend time, effort, or money to develop a campaign in which there are no potential customers. Use only platforms that are often used by your customers and subscribers.

Social Media Marketing can do everything

Social networks today are one of the most important marketing methods. This does not mean that this is the only way of marketing. There are several aspects of your business that you should consider, such as SEO, influence marketing, and branding, if you want to develop a comprehensive marketing strategy. For your campaign to be successful, you need to combine different elements. All elements of your campaign must be fully aligned. Social networks are just one element of your campaign, and you need to combine all the other elements to work together. Traditional marketing methods should be used with new methods. Instead of relying solely on social networks, you should also consider all other aspects.

Facebook is the only option

Social networks are not limited to Facebook,

LinkedIn, or Twitter. Facebook, Instagram, Twitter, and LinkedIn are popular social networking sites, but they are only part of the social networking ecosystem. Web forums, email lists, user groups, various photo and video sharing services, social bookmarking sites, podcasts, and online communities are all part of social networking. You must remember that you must strive to understand the laws that your customers use to communicate and participate.

Chapter 16: Instagram Analytics

In this section, you will learn about how to analyze Instagram analytics and the key data related to your account, along with the most important metrics that you must track.

Instagram has over a billion active users, and more than 400 active users check their Instagram feed daily. Not just the Instagrammers, but even the brands and marketers are going gaga over this wonderful network. It is not only visually appealing and popular but is also a conducive ecosystem for the growth of your personal brand.

In 2019, Instagram has no longer become a mere social media tool but is also a place to develop online communities and a hub for interacting with your audience. If you want to make it big on Instagram, then you must learn to make the most of this platform. It is quintessential that you start looking at Instagram strategically. You might have your account up and running and might have a decent number of followers, however, how do you know if you are using Instagram properly? How do you know if your performance is optimal on Instagram? This is where Instagram analytics steps in. The five most important Instagram metrics that you must track are follower growth, audience demographics, website clicks, reach, and engagement rate.

Before learning about the metrics, you must know what Instagram analytics are. Instagram analytics refers to the way you understand the performance of your posts and your account. Instagram metrics are statistics for specific aspects of your account, whereas Instagram analytics helps you interpret all those statistics and notice any patterns that might exist in them. For instance, your follower count is a metric and the rate of follower growth (how quickly your follower count is growing) is an analytic.

Going through your Instagram analytics is the

best way to determine whether your account is doing well or not. If you review them carefully, then you can obtain useful feedback that will reveal the areas in which you are doing well and the ones you must work on. There are two ways in which you can access your analytics - the first one is by accessing Instagram Insights, and the other option is to use third-party analytics tools. You will learn more about third-party tools in the next chapter.

Instagram Insights is a brilliant way to obtain analytics for your Instagram account. It gives you a variety of data, such as the number of users who viewed your profile in the last couple of days, the time when your followers are usually online...etc., however, to access this you must switch your account to a business profile, or have a lot of engagement.

The main drawback of Instagram's native analytics tools is that the data ranges are quite limited. For most of the metrics, you can at most see how your performance is changing from one week to another. This is the main reason why people tend to opt for third-party analytics tools. Before learning about the different metrics, let us see how you can access Instagram Insights for your account.

You cannot view Instagram Insights on a desktop - you will need a mobile version of the app. Once you open your app, follow the steps listed here.

Open your profile by tapping on the profile picture present on the bottom-right corner of your screen. Tap on the menu option on the screen. Now, tap on the Insights option at the top of the menu (right next to the graph icon). You can now view insights and analytics about the performance of your account. The three tabs you can switch between are Activity, Content, and Audience.

The three main analytics you can view are - Activity, Content, and Audience.

Activity refers to the number of people who have interacted with your content and the number of accounts you have managed to reach with your most recent posts. This tab has two subcategories within it - Interactions and Discovery.

Interactions cover the number of people who have visited your Instagram profile, the number of people who clicked the link in your bio, and the number of people who might have asked for directions (if you list an address in your bio). Your total reach and the impressions of your content are covered under Discovery.

The Content tab is related to how well your posts and Stories are performing. There are three subcategories within this section, and they are Feed posts, Promotions, and Stories.

Feed posts reveal how your usual posts are performing. This feature lets you filter your posts based on different metrics like reach, follows, and comments. You can also adjust the timeframe of these performance metrics between the past seven days to up to two years. You can also filter your post based on the format of the post - photo, video, shopping post, or a carousel post. The best part of Insights is the performance options it gives. As with the Feed posts, the Stories section tells you how well your Instagram Stories have been performing using a variety of metrics; however, all you can see are the stats for the timeframe ranging from the last 24 hours to 14 days. The Promotions segment shows you the performance data related to your promoted posts; however, it is better to check for the performance of your promoted posts using a third-party tool since they offer more features.

The final analytics tab is Audience. It gives you the demographics of your audience and shows you their usual habits. It gives you information about your follower count and the ways in which it changed in the previous week. Under the Top Locations section, you can see the top five cities as well as the countries in which the majority of your followers reside. Age range allows you to see the distribution of your followers according to their age, and gender does the same. The most important section of all is the Followers one. It allows you to see the hours or the days of the week when most of your audience is online.

Wow, that's plenty of data, and all the trends that you notice in the metrics will help you change your Instagram tactics to make your account more efficiently. So, what are the best metrics that you can track on Instagram? To improve the quality of the content you post, your profile, and overall Instagram strategy, you must use what you have learned about in your analytics to check what is working for you and what isn't. All this data might be quite overwhelming, and you might not know where to begin. The metrics that you track will primarily depend on the goal you want to achieve using Instagram. All the metrics certainly aren't created equally. There are some that will give you a lot of information about what your best posts are whereas other metrics might not give you any insight whatsoever. Let me make things easier for you by listing the top five metrics that you must concentrate on:

Follower Growth

The number of followers you have on Instagram is certainly a simple metric, but it is quite important. The number of followers you have tends to have an impact on the performance of your account in several different ways. Take a moment to think about it. Do you want the reach of your posts to increase? The more followers you have, the greater your reach will be. Do you want to get more engagement or increase the clicks of your website? For this, you need more people to follow you. Follower growth is an ideal way to measure how healthy your Instagram account is. You should not only track how many followers you have managed to gain over the past couple of weeks, months, or years but also focus on how quickly your follower base is starting to grow. Tracking the rate at which your account is gaining new followers helps measure the overall popularity of your profile.

Follower growth and follower count

It is quintessential that you understand the analytics about the rate of your follower growth instead of just focusing on the number of followers your account has at the moment. For instance, let us assume that your follower growth has increased by 1% in December, by 2% in January and by 8% in February. You can see here that your account might approach viral growth. It means that in February you probably used some Instagram tactic that seems to be doing well for you. If you notice that the follower growth rate was around 8% in December, 2% in January and 1% in February, it means that your account is not expanding, and it might be due to changes you made in your Instagram's content strategy. If your growth rate goes into the negatives, then it means you are losing followers, and that's a warning sign that something is going wrong. Unfortunately, follower growth isn't something that you can access on Instagram Insights. Insights will show you the number of followers your account has gained or lost when compared to the previous week, but it certainly doesn't give specific analytics about your follower growth over time. You have two ways in which you can track this growth: you can manually record the follower count of your account each day, week, or month in a spreadsheet format and calculate the percentage of change, or less cumbersome, use a third-party analytics tool.

Audience Demographics

It is certainly helpful to understand how quickly you are gaining followers, but you must also be aware of who your followers are. You probably want to increase your rate of engagement on posts or increase the traffic to your website, then learn about the demographics of your audience. Only when you understand your audience will you be able to devise better content to ensure that your followers stick around while your account grows. For instance, if you want to be a fashion influencer on Instagram and want to appeal to the GenZ audience, and the majority of your audience seems to be the baby boomers, then that must give you a tip that you need to make some changes to your account. Instagram Insights offers some good analytics about your audience composition. You can see the composition of age and the gender of your followers along with the top five cities and countries they come from according to the follower count. Most of the analytics tools tend to go a step further and offer you in-depth data that will certainly come in handy.

How can you derive value from your audience demographics breakup? If you want to make the most of the insights you receive from audience demographics, then the first thing that you must do is create a persona of your ideal target audience. Who do you want to appeal to? How old are they and where do they reside? What language do they speak? Once you have your target audience in mind, you can use this as a yardstick to check the audience demographics of your account and see how closely your followers resemble your target audience.

If you notice any major disparities between these

two, then it's time to reconsider your content strategy. If you want to make your posts more appealing to your target audience, then what are the changes that you can make to the style and tone of the content you are posting? Even if you don't have a specific audience in mind and you think that your content has a widespread appeal across various demographics, even then audience analytics comes in handy. You can see the composition of your followers and their locations and accordingly alter your content to appeal to those who follow you.

Website Clicks

Website clicks are exactly what they sounds like - it is a metric to check the number of people who clicked on your Instagram account to your website or any other landing page. This is useful only if you have another website or blog you want your followers to check. This is quite crucial for some people and not so relevant for others. If your primary target is to increase your web traffic, conversion, or sales then you need to concentrate on this metric. On the other hand, if your target is to mainly develop a community and increase the awareness of your personal brand, then you don't have to concentrate much on this. Instagram is a brilliant way to generate sales traffic given that its popularity and reach are rapidly increasing. If your profile is getting a lot of website clicks, then it means that you have plenty of visitors to your profile and have a good call-to-action (CTA) button in your bio. If you aren't getting as many clicks as you wished for, then it is time to revamp your CTA and the link in your Instagram bio. You can also direct your visitors to your URL and hype up the landing page by adding content related to it in your posts.

Instagram Reach

Most social media managers will argue that the key performance indicator or the KPI isn't a primary metric to concentrate on, but it certainly helps you measure your brand awareness and the buzz your content is generating. So, what does reach mean on Instagram? It is a metric that tells you about the number of people who have seen your posts. Each Instagram user who views your photos, videos or even Stories is counted as one account reached. You might deem this quite similar to impressions, but impressions and reach are quite different on Instagram.

Impressions are counted whenever your content is viewed whereas reach is counted only once for every unique user. Therefore, I suggest that it is better to look at your reach instead of impressions. Impressions are a vain metric and don't give you an idea about the number of people you can reach. The number of impressions you have will always be greater than your reach while impressions don't give you much information. For instance, if someone scrolls past your post ten times without paying any attention to it, then it will count as ten impressions.

Will impressions help your brand if someone scrolled past your posts once or twice? Well, not likely. If you are interested in knowing how many people have viewed your content, then reach is an accurate measure. Instagram Insights will give you a figure that tells you about the number of accounts you have reached in the previous week under the Activity tab of your account, and it will also show you the number of people your posts reached in a day. You can also check the reach for your individual Stories and posts in the Content tab for various timeframes (just set the filters accordingly).

So, why does reach matter? Reach is an important metric because it tells you about posts that are appearing on other people's feeds. Different factors influence your reach on Instagram, such as the number of people who engaged with your post after seeing it, the time they spent looking at the post, or the time at which you published it. Due to all of this, reach will give you a broad idea of how popular, engaging, and well-timed your posts on Instagram are.

If your posts manage to reach a greater percentage of your followers, then it is a great sign that other users are spending a lot of their time by looking at and engaging with your posts. Or, it can also mean that your posting schedule is clearly working. It can also mean both. If you check your engagement rate, you will not be able to understand any of this.

If you realize that your average post reach is decreasing, then consider your posting time and the number of followers who are online when you post it. Also, you must check whether your engagement numbers are going down or not. This brings me to the next metric.

Engagement Rate

On Instagram, engagement is the most critical metric. It is an excellent way in which you can connect with your followers to start conversations and build a community. These days, Instagram is the platform that has the highest rate of engagement for most brands across different social media platforms. The rate of engagement is the best place to start with for any social media manager or digital marketer to increase the chances of success of their content. Why do they need to do this? Well, the Instagram algorithm is designed so that it rewards posts that have a good engagement rate. A post that comes first on the user's feed will depend on the rate of engagement that post has and how quickly people engaged with the post after it was posted. Instagram does this to generate a positive user experience by giving priority to posts that the users find engaging.

What exactly does engagement mean on Instagram? Engagement refers to the total number of comments, saves, and likes your posts receive. You can see the overall engagement in all your posts by adjusting the filters on the Content tab within Instagram Insights.

Engagement and Engagement Rate on Instagram

What about the engagement rate on Instagram? This is certainly a better metric than engagement to determine how interesting or engaging your posts are. It also shows you the percentage of users who saw your post and engaged with it. For instance, let us assume that one of your posts has a high reach and another one has low reach, but they both have the same amount of engagement. Then, in such a situation, it is safe to assume that the post with low reach was more compelling to your audience since its engagement rate was higher given that it had a low reach. Engagement rate isn't shown in Insights, but you can calculate it rather easily. You simply divide the number of engagements your post received by the total reach of your post, and then multiply it by 100% to get your engagement rate. For instance, let us assume that one of your posts receives 100 engagements, and its reach is 1000. So, your engagement rate is 100/1000 X 100% = 10%.

Chapter 17: Best Analytics Tools for Instagram

Initially, Instagram was a black hole when it came to third-party marketing tools. Now, fast-forward to 2019 and times have certainly changed. From engagement metrics to social listening, you will be spoiled for choice when it comes to third-party Instagram analytics tools. Given that you have plenty of choices, it can be quite tricky to find the best analytics tool for yourself. With the recent surge in the popularity of this platform along with the constant changes made to its algorithm, it can be difficult to find a long-term solution. In this chapter, you will be given a list of the best tools you can use for Instagram analytics in 2019. You can use these analytics tools to transform your account.

However, please note that there is no such thing as a silver bullet when it comes to making it big on Instagram. The platform and its content are so diverse that at times the best thing that you can do is stack up on different analytics tools. Maybe your primary focus is on stories and the content generated by the users. Maybe you run ads or influencer campaigns frequently. Regardless of what your goal is, here is a list of the best Instagram analytics tools that you can use to enhance your data-tracking game immediately.

Sprout Social

This is a great social media management tool for all businesses as well as agencies. Sprout Social certainly has some great analytics features. A user can use this to schedule their Instagram content; it comes with a comprehensive dashboard that gives you a breakdown of your content that's doing extremely well along with your audience growth. These features will help you understand whether your content strategy is doing as well as it is supposed to and if it is supporting your growth on Instagram instead of letting your follower count saturate. For instance, Sprout Social can help you with information about certain videos or user-generated content that is doing exceptionally well. If you are aware of this, then you can accordingly make changes to your content strategy to ensure better performance.

This tool also allows you to see the hashtags that are doing great and gives you an opportunity to experiment with the top-performing hashtags to find the most favorable ones. Perhaps the most noteworthy feature of this application is its Stories analytics. Given that there are over 400 million active users who publish Stories daily, users need to look closely at their Instagram analytics to track content that's doing well. Alongside the regular post metrics, the Stories data it offers will help you see the impressions, reach, taps, and exits your Stories receive. Apart from tracking the performance of your IG Stories, you can also store the metrics from your Instagram account. This allows you to measure and gauge the progress you are making.

Icon Square

This analytics tool is perfect for agencies and brands that have multiple accounts to maintain. This platform offers competitive hashtags and growth-tracking features quite similar to those offered by Sprout Social. This is a full-blown analytics tool and offers a free audit for business profiles on Instagram. With this tool, you can ensure that your profile is fully complete while adhering to the guidelines of Instagram. The audit helps you assess the 30 most recent posts of yours as well as the general settings of your account. Given how competitive Instagram is these days, it never hurts to have a second opinion about your performance.

Phlanx

This is a simple and straightforward tool when compared to the other in-depth analytics tools mentioned in this section. The engagement calculator offered by this tool helps you analyze the engagement rate of your Instagram account. Though this tool is marketed as being ideal for influencers, it is a great tool for all personal and business accounts as well. The rate of engagement is calculated by dividing the total number of likes and comments your post receives by the total number of followers. There is no magic number when it comes to the ideal rate of engagement, but it is good to maintain something in the 3% range. You can also use this tool to track the engagement rate of your competitors along with your own rate. Tools like this help spot any accounts with fake followers and help determine whether the posts are receiving any authentic engagement or not.

TapInfluence

When it comes to influencers, Instagram analytics tools can be used to spot social media influencers directly. This is precisely what TapInfluence does for you. This platform helps analyze a database made up of over 50,000 influencers to help brands find the right accounts for their influencer campaigns. You can narrow down your search based on the industry or even any specific tags according to what you have in mind. This tool also provides a snapshot of different influencers along with their rates and their price per engagement. If you are vetting through influencers to collaborate with, all the data that this platform provides will certainly come in handy. It also provides real-time yardstick reports according to the industry data to help brands or businesses understand how well their influencer campaigns are working.

Curalate

In recent times, there has been a surge in social selling through user-generated content, and this creates a need for an analytics tool that will keep you updated about your best-selling products. You have probably come across some Like2Buy links in bios – these links belong to Curalate. This platform curates user-generated content that enables brands or businesses to sell their products directly through Instagram. The Like2Buy links are all trackable, and you can track the ROI of any social media campaigns. Apart from this, it also offers engagement and sales metrics by monitoring tags and mentions received on posts. A platform like this offers dual functionality – it helps you determine the most valuable content of yours and assess the direct financial returns on any of your campaigns on Instagram.

Union Metrics

This is a great marketing intelligence platform that helps businesses track their own media along with trends in the industry. You have access to a wide range of features, and it also allows you to use the Instagram Account Checkup feature it offers for free. This check-up ensures that you have a detailed report of your top hashtags, most dedicated followers, along with the average engagement of posts. This helps you audit your social media presence for free, and that is certainly a bonus you cannot ignore. Quite similar to the free assessment tool offered by Icon Square, the Union Metrics tool allows you to gain a better understanding of the analytics of your account at a glance.

Bitly

Your Instagram bio is quite valuable. Tracking your bio link is quite important if you want to track the success of your social media campaigns. This comes in handy when you are trying to sell products or are trying to increase the web traffic to your website or any other landing page. This tool is a great tracking tool for growing businesses as well as well-established brands. Are you looking for a way to drive traffic to a specific landing page? Then Bitly will breakdown your clickable links in bio, and you can use it in combination with Google URL builder to obtain an in-depth report about the performance of your campaigns. Apart from bio URLs, you can use this to track links that are included in any of your paid-for Instagram campaigns.

Keyhole

This is a great analytics tool that helps you measure your past performance along with analyzing real-time data. It offers a real-time hashtag-tracking feature for Instagram and is quite perfect for all social media contests, branding campaigns, and other marketing tactics that use hashtags. Apart from seeing the number of times a specific hashtag is used, you can also check the data related to all the top posts that contain your hashtag and the most engaging posts along with other related hashtags. It certainly does good to ensure that you have a couple of new hashtag ideas on hand given that you need about ten hashtags for an optimal rate of engagement on Instagram.

Conclusion

I want to thank you once again for purchasing this book. I hope it proved to be an enjoyable and informative read.

In this book, you were provided all the information that you need for getting started with Instagram and getting ready for the changes in 2019 for effective Instagram marketing. Apart from this, it also provides practical tips and tricks that you can follow to ensure that you are making the most of Instagram to develop your personal brand. Instagram is so much more than a simple picture sharing social media platform. It is one of the most popular and fastest growing social media platforms today and is a great opportunity for self-expression.

Now that you are equipped with all the information that you need, all that's left for you to do is get started as soon as you can. Follow the simple tips, steps, and tricks given in this book to make it big on Instagram.

Thank you and all the best!

Resources

https://www.thedesigntwins.com/how-to-master-instagram-collaboration/

https://thinkcreativecollective.com/blog/how-to-find-collaborate-with-instagram-influencers-to-grow-your-brand

http://thecoffeedate.com/blog/how-to-collab-on-instagram

https://grow.grin.co/collab-ideas-for-instagram/

https://elisedarma.com/blog/ultimate-guide-instagram-influencer

https://www.falcon.io/insights-hub/topics/social-media-strategy/instagram-analytics-metrics-and-insights/

https://sproutsocial.com/insights/instagram-analytics-tools/

https://www.jennstrends.com/10-reasons-why-you-should-be-on-instagram/

https://sociallysorted.com.au/7-reasons-why-i-love-instagram/

https://www.webwise.ie/parents/explained-image-sharing-app-instagram/